C000124767

Edexcel A2 Music
Revision Guide

by
Alistair Wightman

RHINEGOLD
EDUCATION

www.rhinegoldeducation.co.uk

Music Study Guides
GCSE, AS and A2 Music Study Guides (AQA, Edexcel and OCR)
GCSE, AS and A2 Music Listening Tests (AQA, Edexcel and OCR)
GCSE, AS and A2 Music Revision Guides (AQA, Edexcel and OCR)
AS and A2 Music Technology Revision Guides (Edexcel)
AS/A2 Music Technology Study Guide (Edexcel)
AS/A2 Music Technology Listening Tests (Edexcel)

Also available from Rhinegold Education
AS and A2 Music Harmony Workbooks
GCSE and AS Music Composition Workbooks
GCSE and AS Music Literacy Workbooks
Romanticism in Focus, Baroque Music in Focus, Film Music in Focus,
Modernism in Focus, Musicals in Focus
Music Technology from Scratch
Dictionary of Music in Sound

First published 2014 in Great Britain by
Rhinegold Education
14–15 Berners Street
London W1T 3LJ, UK
www.rhinegoldeducation.co.uk

© 2014 Rhinegold Education
a division of Music Sales Limited

You should always check the current requirements of the examination, since these may change.
Copies of the Edexcel specification can be downloaded from the Edexcel website at www.edexcel.com
Telephone: 0845 1720205   Email: publication.orders@edexcel.com

Edexcel A2 Music Revision Guide
Order No. RHG351
ISBN 978-1-78305-582-1

Exclusive Distributors:
Music Sales Ltd
Distribution Centre, Newmarket Road
Bury St Edmunds, Suffolk IP33 3YB, UK

Printed in the EU

Contents

THE AUTHOR

Alistair Wightman read Music at Oxford and then York University, where he was awarded a D. Phil for his study of the music of Karol Szymanowski. He has worked in primary, secondary and further education, and is a freelance teacher and writer as well as principal examiner in history and analysis in A-level music. His publications include *Writing about Music* (Rhinegold Education, 2008) and several books and articles devoted to Tadeusz Baird, Karłowicz and Szymanowski, including *Karłowicz, Young Poland and the Musical Fin-de-siècle* (Ashgate, 1996), *Karol Szymanowski: his Life and Music* (Ashgate, 1999) and *Szymanowski on Music: Selected Writings of Karol Szymanowski* (Toccata Press, 1999).

ACKNOWLEDGEMENTS

The author would like to thank the consultant Hugh Benham and the Rhinegold Education editorial and design team of Matthew Hammond, Harriet Power and Christina Forde for their expert support in the preparation of this book. Thanks also go to Paul Terry who wrote some additional material for this edition.

COPYRIGHT

Introduction

For the Edexcel A2 qualification in Music you have to complete the following parts:

Unit 4: Extended Performance (30% of the total A2 mark)

Unit 5: Composition and Technical Study (30% of the total A2 mark)

Unit 6: Further Musical Understanding (40% of the total A2 mark).

At the start of the summer term, it is quite likely that you will still have to finish Units 4 and 5. Try to complete these assignments as promptly as possible in order to leave more time to revise for the Unit 6 examination.

SET WORKS

This revision guide is designed to help you prepare for Unit 6, an externally-assessed examination that lasts two hours. The paper is divided into three sections, and this guide deals particularly with Sections B (Music in Context) and C (Continuity and Change in Instrumental Music). Some tips are given on pages 7–11 concerning Section A (Aural Analysis), although you will find more coverage on this section, along with test material, in Rhinegold Education's *Edexcel A2 Music Listening Tests* (4th edition).

The mark total for Unit 6 is 90, distributed as follows:

Section A: 28

Section B: 26

Section C: 36

Unit 6

The set works change annually, so make sure that you study the correct music for the year you are taking the examination. All the prescribed works are taken from *The New Anthology of Music* (*NAM*) edited by Julia Winterson (Edexcel, 2008), and details of the requirements for each year are given below. Bear in mind that, though based on music which may well be unfamiliar to you, Section A (Aural Analysis) questions will focus on genres and styles that you have studied for Sections B and C. Note that the specification (syllabus) requires you to study both areas of study prescribed for each year: Applied Music and Instrumental Music.

Applied Music 2015

➤ NAM 7: Stravinsky – *Pulcinella Suite*: 'Sinfonia', 'Gavotta' and 'Vivo'

➤ NAM 14: Gabrieli – *Sonata Pian' e forte*

➤ NAM 36: Purcell – 'Thy Hand, Belinda' and 'When I am Laid In Earth' from *Dido and Aeneas*

➤ NAM 44: Goldsmith – *Planet of the Apes*: 'The Hunt' (opening)

➤ NAM 59: Gong Kebyar de Sebatu (Bali) – *Baris Melampahan*.

Instrumental Music 2015

➤ NAM 6: Tippett – Concerto for Double String Orchestra: movement I

➤ NAM 10: Cage – *Sonatas and Interludes for Prepared Piano*: Sonatas I–III

➤ NAM 15: Corelli – Trio Sonata in D, Op. 3 No. 2: movement IV

➤ NAM 16: Haydn – String Quartet in E♭, Op. 33 No. 2, 'The Joke': movement IV

➤ NAM 17: Beethoven – Septet in E♭, Op. 20: movement I

➤ NAM 23: Schumann – *Kinderscenen*, Op. 15: Nos. 1, 3 and 11

➤ NAM 48: Louis Armstrong and his Hot Five – *West End Blues*.

Applied Music 2016

➤ NAM 28: J. S. Bach – Cantata No. 48, 'Ich elender Mensch': movements I–IV

➤ NAM 40: Schoenberg – 'Der kranke Mond' from *Pierrot Lunaire*

➤ NAM 43: Bernstein – *On the Waterfront*: 'Symphonic Suite' (opening)

➤ NAM 45: John Williams – *ET*: 'Flying Theme'

➤ NAM 61: Niall Keegan (Ireland) – *Tom McElvogue's* (jig) and *New Irish Barndance* (reel).

Instrumental Music 2016

➤ NAM 2: Haydn – Symphony No. 26 in D minor, 'Lamentatione': movement I

➤ NAM 13: Holborne – Pavane 'The image of melancholy' and Galliard 'Ecce quam bonum'

➤ NAM 18: Brahms – Piano Quintet in F minor, Op. 34: movement III

➤ NAM 21: J. S. Bach – Partita No. 4 in D, BWV 828: Sarabande and Gigue

➤ NAM 25: Shostakovich – Prelude and Fugue in A, Op. 87 No. 7

➤ NAM 49: Duke Ellington and his Orchestra – *Black and Tan Fantasy*

➤ NAM 50: Miles Davis Quintet – *Four* (opening).

Applied Music 2017

➤ NAM 7: Stravinsky – *Pulcinella Suite*: 'Sinfonia', 'Gavotta, and 'Vivo'

➤ NAM 27: Gabrieli – *In ecclesiis*

➤ NAM 42: Auric – *Passport to Pimlico*: 'The Siege of Burgundy'

➤ NAM 46: Pheloung – *Morse on the Case*

➤ NAM 62: Mustapha Tettey Addy (Ghana) – *Agbekor Dance.*

Instrumental Music 2017

➤ NAM 3: Berlioz – *Harold in Italy*: movement III

➤ NAM 9: Shostakovich – String Quartet No. 8, Op. 110: movement I

➤ NAM 10: Cage – *Sonatas and Interludes for Prepared Piano*: Sonatas I–III

➤ NAM 15: Corelli – Trio Sonata in D, Op. 3 No. 2: movement IV

➤ NAM 20: Sweelinck – *Pavana Lachrimae*

➤ NAM 22: Mozart – Piano Sonata in B♭, K. 333: movement I

➤ NAM 58: Ram Narayan (India) – *Rag Bhairav.*

All works listed in both sections for each year must be tackled, as Section B (Music in Context) draws on the Applied Music list, and Section C (Continuity and Change) on the Instrumental Music list.

SECTION A (AURAL ANALYSIS)

There are two questions in this section of the examination:

1. Comparison of two excerpts of music without reference to notation

2. A general test of aural perception, involving notation of a melody (both pitch and rhythm), identifying specific compositional devices (keys, chords and cadences), and providing information on the historical context. For this question a skeleton score is provided.

You should practise as frequently and as regularly as possible, ensuring that you form the habit of:

•   Noting the number of marks there are (and therefore how much information is required) for each question, or part of question

•   Working out plausible possibilities (e.g. related keys) to support your impressions

- Understanding and using correct terminology (keep referring to the glossary at the end of this guide)

- In the comparison question, be prepared to answer questions on:
  - Instruments and/or voices
  - Textures
  - Rhythmic devices and patterns
  - Melodic aspects
  - Features of word-setting
  - Historical context (i.e. genre, composer, date of composition).

The historical context questions may well be multiple choice. If you are not sure about the genre, try to match the excerpts to the set works you have studied. Try hard, also, to relate the date of composition to the composer you have selected. If the question about the date is open-ended – i.e., you are invited to suggest a date yourself – try to be reasonably precise. For example, if you believe the composer is Bach, it is better to suggest '1720' rather than '18th century'.

> Useful resources are the Sample Assessment Materials (Edexcel, 2007, publications code UA018895) and *Edexcel A2 Music Listening Tests, 4th edition* (Rhinegold Education, 2014).

Keys

Prediction of plausible possibilities could be especially helpful in the general test of aural perception. Before you hear the music played, use the skeleton score to identify the key at the opening, after which you can work out the five related keys (as specified in Edexcel's *Tutor Support Materials*) to which the music may modulate. Notice that the question will be restricted to just these possibilities.

The possibilities are as follows for an excerpt starting in a major key:

	Relative minor
Dominant	Relative minor of dominant
Subdominant	Relative minor of subdominant

For an excerpt starting in a minor key, the possibilities are:

	Relative major
Dominant	Relative major of dominant
Subdominant	Relative major of subdominant

In the case of music in the key of C major, for example, the range of possible modulations are:

	A minor (relative minor)
G major (dominant)	E minor (relative minor of the dominant)
F major (subdominant)	D minor (relative minor of the subdominant)

If the music is in C minor, the modulations will involve:

	E♭ major (relative major)
G minor (dominant)	B♭ major (relative major of the dominant)
F minor (subdominant)	A♭ major (relative major of the subdominant)

As a practice drill for this question, work out as quickly as possible the five related keys for all keys up to and including four sharps or flats (it is unlikely that a test involving more accidentals than this would be set in an exam).

Cadences

You are almost sure to be asked to identify cadences, especially in the general test of aural perception.

If you are not yet entirely confident about coping with cadences, try to remember the following points and develop a 'feel' for the effects they produce.

1. **Perfect** cadence: chord V–chord I

    There should be a closed or complete feel to the music at the point this cadence occurs. The key may have changed, of course, but whatever the context, the perfect cadence will give the impression of coming to the end of an individual statement, even though the music may move on. Such situations are perhaps analogous to the use of full stops part-way through a paragraph.

2. **Imperfect** cadence: finishes with chord V

    This cadence should give an open, incomplete feel, similar to a comma or semi-colon in a sentence.

3. **Interrupted** cadence: chord V–chord VI (most frequently)

    This is perhaps best regarded as a sort of derailed perfect cadence. Expectations are defeated by avoidance of the tonic, most frequently but not invariably through the use of chord VI.

4. **Plagal** cadence: chord IV–chord I

    Often likened to the church 'Amen', this results in a less emphatic return to the tonic chord, and is far less frequently heard.

Chords

The aural perception test can involve identification of any chord, but it is likely that at A2 level questions will involve some chromatic harmony. Study the numbered examples in the extract below from Mozart's Piano Sonata, K. 284. Remember, however, that it is really important that you not only recognise the chords on paper, but also that you develop the ability to recognise the sound of them. As ever,

> Two different types of augmented 6th chord figure in these examples. We have named them here, but in the exam it is enough to describe them just as augmented 6ths.

the context is all-important (for example, it is frequently the case that the Neapolitan 6th substitutes for chord IIb preceding a cadence, just as augmented 6th chords often pave the way for a dominant chord or tonic chord in its second inversion).

1.   (Italian) Augmented 6th chord. Note how it paves
      the way for progression Ic–V in D minor.

2.   (German) Augmented 6th chord. Leading to Ic–V^7–I
      in A minor.

3.   Diminished 7ths on first and third crotchets of
      the bar.

> For further information on all
> these points, consult the *A2
> Music Harmony Workbook*
> by Hugh Benham (Rhinegold
> Education, 2008).

4.   Neapolitan 6th. Try to recognise the intensified plangent, 'weepy' sound.

5.   (Italian) Augmented 6th preceding Ic–V^7–I in D minor.

Other harmonic devices

You may also be asked to identify such common features as the following:

➢   Pedal point (you may have to state whether it is a tonic or dominant pedal)

➢   Suspension

➢   Appoggiatura

➢   False relation

➢   Tierce de Picardie.

> See the glossary for
> definitions.

Finally, remember that in examinations you find yourself in an artificial situation. You are often tested on the various skills you learn separately, but in spite of this try not to let your own approach become rigidly compartmentalised. Try to appreciate musical works as a whole, and apply the knowledge you gain in one area of your activities to other aspects of your musical investigations. For example, your study of harmony should also help your listening and your exploration of musical styles.

SECTIONS B AND C

The rest of this guide is aimed at helping you to:

➢   Organise the information you have already collected (and may still be collecting)

➢   Focus on the demands of questions which are set in this exam

➢   Improve the way you express your ideas.

You must take an unmarked copy of the Anthology into the exam, and this in itself is a valuable aid to you if you can find your way round the scores quickly and efficiently. It will help if you **keep listening to your prescribed works** so that you begin to recognise and locate the key features we shall be looking at. Obviously, it makes much more sense to be able to locate features you require in the score itself than to try to memorise abstract accounts of the work.

Demands of Sections B and C

In Section B, you answer two out of three options, all dealing with music in context. In other words, the questions will involve showing how features of musical style relate to the historical background or the purpose of the work. The works are all taken from the Applied Music list, and by definition have some sort of function (e.g. incidental music, music for opera, or music for some sort of ceremony).

In Section B you may answer in note form if you prefer, without the risk of incurring any penalty. Each option is worth 13 marks, giving a total of 26 for the section. Do not waste time answering a third option as well – you won't gain any more marks, and may not leave yourself enough time to produce a well-written essay for Section C.

In Section C, you must answer one question of the two set on Instrumental Music. You should write in continuous prose, as your essay will be assessed both for the information it contains and the way you have expressed yourself.

The total mark for the essay is 36, and we shall see how the marks are allocated in the sample essays that can be found towards the end of this book.

In Edexcel's Sample Assessment Materials you will find holistic descriptors for each question set in both Sections B and C. The examiners will naturally take into account the number of correct, relevant and valid points you make. They will also assess the quality of the writing (Quality of Written Communication – QWC), and this will involve such aspects as:

> The holistic descriptors are based on a hierarchy of words – from 'Outstanding' to 'Poor' – each with a range of marks and a brief description of the attributes expected in an answer at that level.

➤ Organisation, planning and coherence

➤ Syntax and spelling

➤ Use of appropriate terminology.

We have already stated that you may answer in note form in Section B if you wish. You will, however, have to be careful to express yourself as clearly as possible, arranging your points in a logical, coherent sequence.

On pages 14–80 are **revision notes** for each of the set works, giving a brief historical context, followed by a series of pointers to the most important technical features of the music: rhythm and metre, melody, harmony, tonality, texture, performance resources and structure.

We have also provided examples of **questions, mark schemes (indicative content) and specimen answers with commentaries** for you to study. Some answers have been left unmarked for you to evaluate. In addition we have suggested short exercises aimed at helping you to improve the way you present your ideas.

Naturally, you will be most interested in the set works for your year, but find time to glance at the remaining specimen answers, as suggestions are made throughout this section on how to improve the quality of your written communication.

One of the most common reasons for losing marks is irrelevance. Always stick to the point and write about the works specified in the question.

Do not worry if, sometimes, you seem to be stating the obvious! And, where possible, always try to provide at least one example for each point you make, though in some cases more than one example would be desirable. For example, if the question concerns tonality then you should try to give as much detail as possible about how the composer modulates right the way through the piece. Many candidates fail to earn high marks because they neglect to pursue the line of enquiry as thoroughly as possible.

Think about how best to organise your time when answering questions. You do not have to worry about Section A, as the instructions and extracts on the CD dictate timings for you. For the rest of the paper, for which you will probably have approximately an hour and a half, you could allow yourself roughly 20 minutes for each of the sub-sections you select in Section B, and about 50 minutes for the Section C essay. Try to allow some time for reading through your work before handing in your answer book.

Useful additional reading:

➤ *Dictionary of Music in Sound* by David Bowman (Rhinegold Education, 2002)

➤ *Writing about Music Workbook* by Alistair Wightman (Rhinegold Education, 2008)

➤ *Edexcel A2 Music Study Guide* by David Bowman and Paul Terry (Rhinegold Education, 2014).

Revision notes

Below, we have provided a series of points that should help you to focus on the most important aspects of each of the works set for the year in which you are taking the examination. It would not be wise to try to memorise everything for a parrot-like recitation of facts and figures. We suggest you check that you understand the main points, or generalisations, given under the various headings. After this, try to absorb some of the additional points – these should help you to think of your own examples which can be used to illustrate the work in question.

It is most important that you keep referring to the Anthology, and associate the points made in the following lists with **what you hear in the music and see on the score**. Attempting to learn these points in the form of abstract crib notes means you do not get anything out of the exercise in the long term, and also run the risk of error.

We have also made one or two suggestions for further listening. While by no means essential, it would help you to broaden your acquaintance with the composer or type of music in question, and hopefully aid you in the listening section of the examination.

APPLIED MUSIC 2015

Stravinsky – *Pulcinella Suite*: 'Sinfonia', 'Gavotta' and 'Vivo'

Background	
	• First performed on 15 May 1920 at the Paris Opéra
	• Commissioned by Serge Diaghilev, the impresario who founded the Ballets Russes
	• In contrast to the huge orchestral demands of the ballet scores of the years preceding World War I (such as *Petrushka* and *The Rite of Spring*), *Pulcinella's* relatively modest demands are indicative of the reduced scale of Diaghilev's post-war enterprises.
	• This work is neoclassical in style:
	• It reflects a reaction against the emotionalism and 'giganticism' of late-Romantic music
	• It uses 18th-century models
	• The Sinfonia is based on music by Gallo
	• The Gavotta is extracted from keyboard variations by Monza
	• The Vivo is built on a cello sonata by Pergolesi.
	• Stravinsky goes further than arranging his 18th-century materials; instead, though retaining the broad outlines of the originals, he 'recomposes' them.

Rhythm and metre	The basic rhythmic schemes and metres are disrupted by: • Heavy off-beat accents (e.g. Vivo, bar 33) • Persistent syncopation (e.g. Sinfonia, bars 17–18 in violin II) • Bars with differing time signatures (e.g. Sinfonia, bars 10–12) • Introduction of long sustained notes at odds with 'foreground' music (e.g. Sinfonia, bars 7–9) • Irregular groupings of shorter notes (e.g. Gavotta, groups of 5 (bar 27), 9 (bar 31), 11 (bar 73), 12 (bar 78)).
Melody	Compared to the other musical elements, melody is more recognisably similar to the original sources, although Stravinsky does introduce: • Blurred outlines through glissandi (e.g. Vivo, bar 2, trombone) • Extensive 'non-Baroque' ornamentation (e.g. Gavotta, bar 83, flute 1).
Harmony	Disruptions here include: • The introduction of additional notes to result in 'wrong-note' harmony (e.g. the added 9th in the violin II part in bar 3 of the Sinfonia) • The combination of G and D major chords at bar 44 (beat 1) of the Gavotta • A loud tonic-over-dominant chord at bar 33 of the Vivo:  • Use of folk-style drones in unexpected contexts (e.g. Sinfonia, violin II, bars 17–18) • Weakening of bass lines (e.g. Sinfonia, bar 43 – sudden drop in volume and removal of double bass from the texture) • Unexpected cadences (e.g. III–I at end of the Vivo).
Texture and scoring	The original pieces were taken from chamber music or keyboard sources, thus allowing considerable freedom in orchestration and texture: • There is no continuo • The solo quintet in the Sinfonia and Vivo may have been suggested by the Baroque concerto grosso (but if so is a highly unusual 'concertino' grouping) • The solo trombone in the Vivo, with glissandi, is a 20th-century touch • As is the high double-bass solo in the Vivo

- The Gavotta is scored for wind instruments only, reflecting Stravinsky's increasing preference for such sonorities (e.g. *Symphonies for Wind Instruments*, *Concerto for Piano and Winds*).

Textures, though predominantly melody-dominated homophony, are highly contrasting:

- Loosely imitative wind writing at bars 6–10 of the Sinfonia

- Melody and drone at bars 17–18 of the Sinfonia

- Sustained chords in the solo quintet, supported by repeated chords in the main part of the orchestra (bars 37–39 of the Sinfonia)

- Two-part oboe and horn writing at the start of Variation I of the Gavotta

- Quasi-Alberti bass in the bassoons in Variation II

- Unison statement of the main theme at start of the Vivo

- Heterophony between flutes and trumpet from bar 38 of the Vivo.

> Alberti bass is a particular form of broken-chord accompaniment in which the figuration consists of a recurring four-note pattern in the order low-high-middle-high:
>
>

Structure and tonality	- These aspects of the music afford the clearest evidence of its stylistic origins in the 18th century
	- The Sinfonia is in rounded binary form (with the A section as bars 1–15 and B section bars 16–44); or else it is an abbreviated ritornello form, with the ritornello theme appearing at bar 1 in G, bar 16 in D, and bar 35 in G
	- Modulations to B minor (bar 26), E minor (bar 29) and A minor (bar 31), as well as use of the circle of 5ths progression, are as expected in 18th-century music
	- The Gavotta is in binary form, and goes on to include only two of the six variations Monza wrote
	- The first part modulates from D to A (bar 10), then to G (bar 14), then briefly through A (bar 18), F♯ minor (bar 20), E minor (bar 22), then to D (bar 24 to the end)
	- The Vivo is in rounded binary form, with modulations from F to C at the end of the first section (bar 21), and to the tonic minor (bar 46)
	- Stravinsky departs from the original by inserting three bars at the start of the second section (bars 22–24).
Further listening	- The rest of the *Pulcinella Suite*
	- *Symphony of Psalms*: movement III (NAM 31)
	- *Petrushka* (an example of Stravinsky's early Russian nationalist style).

Gabrieli – *Sonata pian' e forte*

Background	• The sonata was published in 1597
	• It was probably intended for performance in St Mark's Basilica, Venice on an important liturgical occasion
	• The fact that Gabrieli could call on the services of a relatively large number of instrumentalists is indicative of the wealth of the institution
	• Performance in this building would permit use of the spatially separated galleries for the two four-part groups
	• The work is historically important because it was one of the earliest to specify dynamic contrasts.
Rhythm and metre	• The sonata adopts the well-established procedure of progressing from sedate, longer note values at the start to much livelier movement towards the end
	• Time signatures have been inserted editorially. Most of the piece is notated in duple time, with occasional $\frac{3}{2}$ bars
	• Typical devices include syncopation and dotted rhythms.
Melody	• The melodic style gives the impression of a transfer of motet-like vocal writing to instruments
	• Consequently the ranges are relatively restricted
	• Much of the writing is conjunct, with the largest interval being an octave
	• 4ths and 5ths also occur relatively frequently.
Harmony	• Root-position and first-inversion chords dominate, with the occasional consonant 4th:
	• The writing is not functional but cadences are frequent, including perfect, imperfect (Phrygian) and plagal
	• Typical devices include suspensions (e.g. bar 4), circle of 5ths (e.g bars 36–41) and tierces de Picardie (e.g. bar 80).
Tonality	• The music is based on the Dorian mode on G, but cadences on most steps of the mode contribute to the work's fluid tonal scheme.
Structure	• The sonata is through-composed with clear breaks into contrasting sections

	• The only repetitions occur within sections, often in antiphony, e.g. at bar 34 where the music of bar 31 is repeated a 4th lower.

Texture	• The sonata requires two four-part instrumental groups
	
	• The textures include:
	
	   • Free counterpoint for four parts (e.g. most of bars 1–13)
	
	   • Imitation (e.g. bars 17–20)
	
	   • Antiphony (e.g. bars 37–40)
	
	   • Eight-part counterpoint (e.g. bars 26–31)
	
	   • Eight-part homophony (e.g. bar 40).

Further listening	• Gabrieli – *In ecclesiis* (NAM 27) • Gabrieli – the CD *Music for Brass Volume 1* (Naxos 8.553609), which includes another version of *Sonata pian' e forte*.

Purcell – 'Thy hand, Belinda' and 'When I am laid in earth' from *Dido and Aeneas*

Background	• Henry Purcell was one of the most important English Baroque composers, who worked in the second half of the 17th century • *Dido and Aeneas* was one of the first English operas: it was performed in Chelsea in 1689, but may have been composed for an earlier production at court, possibly to celebrate the coronation of King William III and Queen Mary • No score from Purcell's time survives and some of the music of the opera has been lost • The libretto is based on a play by Nahum Tate, which he adapted from part of the *Aeneid* (written by Virgil around 25 BC) • 'Thy hand, Belinda' is a recitative: recitative is a type of vocal music that follows the rhythms and accents of speech, and is typically used to convey action • 'When I am laid in earth' is an aria: an aria (song) provides a soloist with an opportunity to reflect on the situation in the plot • *Dido and Aeneas* has three acts and lasts just over one hour. It includes choruses, duets and dances, as well as recitatives and arias. This excerpt comes just before the final chorus when Dido, heartbroken that Aeneas has left, prepares to kill herself • 'When I am laid in earth' is often called 'Dido's lament'.

Rhythm and metre	• The time signature of **C** for the recitative is simple quadruple metre (four crotchet beats in a bar)
	• Rhythm of the voice part is flexible in performance, being determined by the words
	• Short phrases are separated by rests
	• In contrast, the accompaniment is very sustained.
	• The aria is in slow $\frac{3}{2}$ time – simple triple metre (three minim beats in a bar).
	• The repeating bass part features a long–short pattern in most bars and is continuous throughout
	• The vocal part contains occasional dotted patterns and rests between many of its phrases.
Melody	• The vocal line of the recitative descends an octave in a mainly stepwise and chromatic fashion
	• The aria is built on a five-bar bass melody that repeats throughout.
	• The vocal line is mainly stepwise, but there are expressive downward leaps on the word 'trouble' and a climactic upward leap to a top G on 'remember me'
	• While the bass is chromatic, the vocal melody is mainly diatonic
	• Violins play descending chromatic lines in the final bars after the singing ceases.
Word setting	• Mainly syllabic, but with short melismas on 'darkness' in the recitative, and on 'laid' and 'ah!' in the aria
	• Purcell makes extensive use of word-painting in the recitative, for example:
	• The rapid modulations give an unsettled feel to portray Dido's anguish
	• False relations between A♮ and A♭, and a melisma suggest the disorientation of darkness
	• Searing chromaticism, dissonances against the bass, short, breathless phrases and a falling musical line all illustrate Dido contemplating suicide
	• A descent toward the bottom of the soprano range occurs as her thoughts turn to death.
	• In the aria the word-painting includes:
	• The expressive falling 5th for 'trouble', spanning a diminished 5th (or tritone) on the first of each of its paired repetitions
	• The declamatory style of 'remember me'
	• Expressive melismas on 'ah!'
	• Minor key
	• Oppressively repeating bass of the entire lament.

Harmony and tonality	• The short recitative passes rapidly through several keys, giving a deliberately unsettled sense of tonality before ending with a Phrygian cadence (IVb–V) in G minor
	• Recitative leads without break into the aria, in G minor throughout, with a number of chromatic passages
	• Most chords are triads in root position or inversion, with occasional 7ths. The excerpt ends with an open 5th (G and D) on the tonic
	• The use of suspensions creates expressive dissonances on the first beat of many bars, the resolutions of which create an impression of sighing to add to the melancholy mood.
Structure	• 'Thy hand, Belinda' is a free-flowing recitative
	• 'When I am laid in earth' is a ground-bass aria; the bass consists of a five-bar ostinato heard 11 times
	• The voice enters after one complete bass pattern with a melody that falls into two halves, each consisting of ten bars that are repeated (AABB – the B section begins with 'Remember me'). The aria ends with an instrumental coda (labelled *ritornelle*) above the last two statements of the bass
	• This type of slow, minor key, triple-time movement over a ground bass is known as a passacaglia
	• The chromatic descent of the bass from tonic to dominant was common in 17th-century ground bass laments. Purcell's genius lies in adopting an unusual five-bar length for his ostinato bass, and in writing vocal phrases which often overlap the bass phrases instead of coinciding with them (e.g. the first vocal phrase is four bars in length and the next vocal phrase begins before the five-bar bass pattern has ended). These overlaps carry the music forward and avoid predictable, regular cadences at the end of every statement of the bass pattern.
Resources	• Soprano voice and string ensemble (1st and 2nd violins, viola and continuo) – a small orchestra typical of the mid-Baroque period
	• The continuo (found in most Baroque ensemble music) consists of at least one bass instrument, such as a cello, and one chordal instrument, such as a harpsichord or archlute. The players of chordal instruments use the figures below the bass part notes ('figured bass') as a guide to filling in the harmonies
	• In the recitative the voice is accompanied only by the continuo
	• Strings join in for the aria – their parts are simple and are kept to a low register (below the voice) until the last 10 bars.
Texture	• Mainly melody-dominated homophony
	• The imitative entries in the *ritornelle* (coda) provide a brief passage of counterpoint.
Further listening	• Purcell – 'The Triumphing Dance' from Act I of *Dido and Aeneas*
	• Purcell – 'Sound the trumpet' from *Come Ye Sons of Art*

Goldsmith – *Planet of the Apes*: 'The Hunt' (opening)

Background	• The score was composed in 1968
	• The film's futuristic content is reflected in the use of 20th-century musical techniques, e.g. the serialism evident in this excerpt
	• The alien atmosphere is conveyed by the use of additional unconventional instruments, some electronic.
Rhythm and metre	• The excerpt is characterised by driving rhythms, opening in $\frac{3}{4}$ and later involving $\frac{4}{4}$
	• There are also occasional $\frac{5}{4}$ bars
	• Typical features include:
	• Heavy stresses
	• A melody marked by long notes followed by much shorter lengths
	• Cross-rhythm of $\frac{6}{8}$ in percussion over $\frac{3}{4}$ in piano and violin II (bar 16)
	• Triplet crotchets against four quavers (bar 42)
	• Syncopation on the ram's horn (bar 52)
	• Polyrhythms (bar 56)
	• $\frac{4}{4}$ in flute and violin I superimposed with $\frac{8}{8}$ in piano and violin II (bar 84).
Melody	• Melodic lines are in general disjunct and chromatic
	• Melodic content is linked to the 12-tone motif (e.g. bars 8–9)
	• Goldsmith draws on component intervals from this line (e.g. flute in bars 13–14)
	• There is some manipulation of lines using serial methods (notice that in the examples below, the basic intervals of the row are often inverted or displaced by an octave):
	• The bass in bar 23 is a (transposed) retrograde of bars 8–9
	• The bass in bars 27–29 is a (transposed) retrograde inversion
	• The bass in bars 32–34 is a (transposed) inversion.

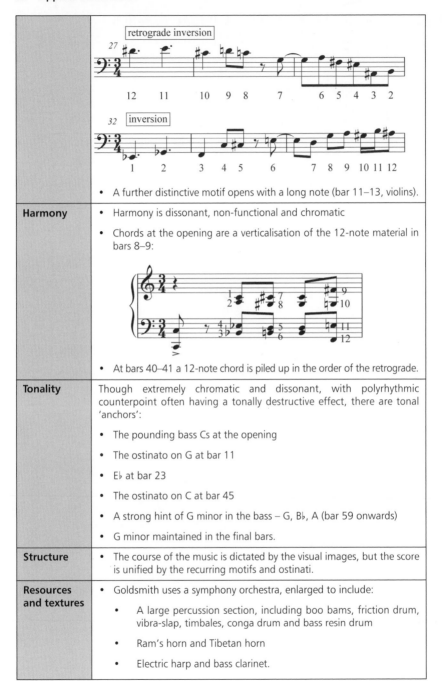

	• A further distinctive motif opens with a long note (bar 11–13, violins).
Harmony	• Harmony is dissonant, non-functional and chromatic
	• Chords at the opening are a verticalisation of the 12-note material in bars 8–9:
	• At bars 40–41 a 12-note chord is piled up in the order of the retrograde.
Tonality	Though extremely chromatic and dissonant, with polyrhythmic counterpoint often having a tonally destructive effect, there are tonal 'anchors':
	• The pounding bass Cs at the opening
	• The ostinato on G at bar 11
	• E♭ at bar 23
	• The ostinato on C at bar 45
	• A strong hint of G minor in the bass – G, B♭, A (bar 59 onwards)
	• G minor maintained in the final bars.
Structure	• The course of the music is dictated by the visual images, but the score is unified by the recurring motifs and ostinati.
Resources and textures	• Goldsmith uses a symphony orchestra, enlarged to include:
	• A large percussion section, including boo bams, friction drum, vibra-slap, timbales, conga drum and bass resin drum
	• Ram's horn and Tibetan horn
	• Electric harp and bass clarinet.

	• Orchestral writing is characterised by the use of extreme ranges
	
	• Textures include:
	
	    • Homophony (e.g. bars 1–3)
	
	    • Ostinato and melody (e.g. bars 11–22)
	
	    • Polyrhythms (e.g. bars 56)
	
	    • Two-part counterpoint (e.g. bars 75–83).

Further listening	• Try viewing any other film with music by Goldsmith, e.g. *Chinatown* (1974) or *The Omen* (1976).

Gong Kebyar de Sabatu (Bali) – *Baris Melampahan*

Background	• Balinese gamelan performance requires a large ensemble of performers playing mostly tuned gongs and metallophones • The instruments are the property of the community rather than the individual members • Baris style is typical of a ritual dance performed by Balinese men to show warlike skills • This excerpt is in *gong kebyar* style.
Rhythm and metre	• There is a regular pulse throughout until the piece slows down at the end • Gong strokes mark the end of each rhythmic cycle (gongan) • The gongan is made up of four-beat ketegs • Throughout the extract, there is a constant 'on-beat' pulse with some 'off-beat' sounds from the reyong • Kendhang rhythms are occasionally displaced.
Melody	• The excerpt is based on a nuclear melody, built on a limited number of pitches from the pelog (selisir) scale • It is heard in varying degrees of completion • The only significant departure occurs at [H], the 'High tune'.
Harmony and tonality	• There is no harmonic progression as such • A sense of tonality results from repetitions of the pelog-derived material.
Structure	• The excerpt consists of alternations of a limited amount of musical material • Structural divisions are stressed by markers from the gong and extreme contrasts of dynamics

> In this context, 'nuclear' denotes the fundamental melodic material for the entire excerpt.

	• Sections are also clearly delineated by the addition or subtraction of forces, e.g. the angsel is marked by the addition of the reyong (gong chimes) and the kendhang (drums).
Timbre, functions and texture	• The only non-percussion instrument is the flute-like suling
	• The remaining instruments consist of gongs, metallophones and unpitched percussion
	• Gongs are deliberately pitched slightly differently to produce ombak (or acoustic 'beat') in tuning
	• Gongs are used to mark the end of rhythmic cycles
	• Metallophones provide melodic content
	• The texture is heterophonic.
Further listening	• The CD *Bali: Gamelan and Kecak*, recorded in Bali by David Lewiston, from Nonesuch Records.

INSTRUMENTAL MUSIC 2015

Tippett – Concerto for Double String Orchestra: movement I

Background	• Concerto for Double String Orchestra is a characteristic work of Tippett's early period
	• Its origins reflect his social concerns
	• It was first performed by the South London Orchestra, founded in the 1930s to provide performance opportunities for unemployed musicians
	• The work was first performed in 1940 at Morley College, Lambeth, where Tippett was musical director
	• As an early work, it reflects Tippett's interests in English madrigals (evident in freely combining independent rhythmic patterns) and Neoclassicism, a movement associated with Stravinsky.
Rhythm and metre	• Notated in $\frac{8}{8}$, with very occasional changes to $\frac{6}{8}$ and $\frac{4}{8}$
	• The use of quavers as the basic unit permits additive rhythms
	• Syncopation is frequent, with rhythmic patterns extending over the barline
	• Only at bar 95 does the music settle into a 'regular' crotchet pulse
	• Here Tippett introduces rhythmic augmentation, i.e. the motif opening with crotchets in violin 1, orchestra 1 is doubled in length at bar 99 (cellos, orchestra 1) and doubled again at bar 103 (viola and cellos of orchestra 2, where the initial pitch plus rests takes up a whole bar).
Melody	• Opening motif characterised by repeated step movement before broadening out by leaps of 4th and 3rd

	• Melody extended by sequence (bar 8)
	• Melody here is also inverted in lower parts
	• Transition material marked by a more cantabile approach, with longer note-lengths and appearance of trills
	• Prominent broken-chord motif in bass at bar 112.
Harmony	• Non-functional
	• Harmonic progressions are difficult to discern for the most part because of the lean contrapuntal textures
	• Counterpoint leads to dissonant collisions
	• The more obvious harmonic 'events' include:
	• Phrygian cadence at bars 20–21
	• Common chord progression at bars 39–40
	• Ambiguous progression from bar 119 with augmented/whole-tone structures heard in passing
	• Final modal cadence of G to A, or tonic preceded by flattened seventh.
Tonality	• On A
	• Non-functional, with modal elements
	• Bars 1–4 of melody use the pentatonic scale, but accidentals in other parts make it more difficult to be certain which mode predominates
	• Tippett shifts the music to various tonal areas, e.g.
	• G (bars 39–67)
	• E (bar 68)
	• C♯ (bar 86)
	• A♭ (bar 107)
	• A (bar 129).
	• The movement closes with an open 5th chord.
Structure	• The regular appearance of the opening motif is reminiscent of the ritornello of the Baroque concerto grosso
	• The overall structure, however, is sonata form
	• There are two clearly defined subjects (bar 1, bar 39) linked by a transition (bar 21)
	• The development (bar 68) passes through more remote tonal areas (see above)
	• The opening material reappears in a recapitulation (bar 129), with the second subject in the home tonality of A as opposed to the original G
	• There is an extended coda (bar 194), which eventually reaffirms the home tonality.

Resources/ Texture	• This concerto plays two equal forces off against each other, rather than a single soloist or group of soloists against a larger accompanying group
	• Tippett frequently uses two-part counterpoint, as in the main theme, but each part is doubled at three octaves
	• He also uses occasional homophony and monophony, as well as antiphony
	• In the more lyrical sections, the accompaniment sometimes takes the form of broken chords
	• There are no unconventional playing techniques, but notice the 'sul tasto' (bow over the fingerboard) direction at bar 107.

Cage – *Sonatas and Interludes for Prepared Piano*: Sonatas I–III

Background	• The Sonatas are taken from a cycle of 16 sonatas and four interludes, completed in 1948
	• They are one of a series of works written for prepared piano (see instructions preceding the Sonatas in the Anthology for information on how the piano is 'prepared')
	• The prepared piano originated when Cage was commissioned to compose a dance piece for Syvilla Fort in 1940
	• The performing venue was so restricted that Cage could only use a piano, and therefore had to expand on the range of sounds available to him from the one instrument he could use
	• The works of these years also reflect the composer's interest in Indian philosophy, and the idea of the 'permanent emotions'
	• Because of preparation, the most important musical elements for the listener involve rhythm, structure, texture and timbre.
Rhythm and metre	• With the fractal/micro-macrocosmic scheme, small-scale rhythmic durations determine the overall proportions of the structure
	• Sonata I uses seven-crotchet units in sets of 4–1–3 (repeated) and 4–2 (repeated):

Bars 1–7	$4 \times 7 =$ duration of 28 crotchets
Bar 8	$1 \times 7 =$ duration of 7 crotchets
Bars 9–12	$3 \times 7 =$ duration of 21 crotchets
Bars 13–19	$4 \times 7 =$ duration of 28 crotchets
Bars 20–26	$2 \times 7 = 14$ crotchets

• Sonata II uses 31-crotchet units in sets of 1½ (repeated) and 2⅜ (repeated):

	Bars 1–14	1½ x 31 = duration of 46½ crotchets
	Bars 15–37	2⅜ x 31 = duration of 53½ crotchets (approximately)

- Sonata III uses 34-crotchet units in sets of 1 (repeated) and 3¼ (repeated):

	Bars 1–8	1 x 34 = duration of 34 crotchets
	Bars 9–32	3¼ x 34 = duration of 110½ crotchets

- At surface level, the Sonatas are marked by:

  - Off-beat effects

  - Triplets

  - Other irregular note groupings

  - Rhythmic displacements of short patterns (although Sonata III makes use of a more regular pulse)

- There are frequent changes of time signature.

Melody	<ul><li>The usual features of melody are difficult to discern because of the distortion of pitch through the piano's preparations</li><li>There are some apparently chromatic and pentatonic elements</li><li>Elsewhere, lines are often angular.</li></ul>
Harmony	<ul><li>Traditional harmonic procedures are impossible because of the effects of preparation</li><li>There are no cadences, and only occasional discernible chord structures:<ul><li>The opening 7th chord of Sonata I</li><li>The parallel chords at bars 20–23 of Sonata I.</li></ul></li></ul>
Tonality	<ul><li>It is not useful to speak of tonality in relation to these works, although Cage occasionally uses procedures which have a tonal function in traditional music – e.g. the pedal in the left-hand part at the opening of Sonata III, notated as an A but usually sounding as C.</li></ul>
Structure	<ul><li>The Sonatas are superficially in binary form with repeats and some recapitulation (e.g. Sonata I, bar 18)</li><li>The organisation is fundamentally rhythmic (see above).</li></ul>
Texture and timbre	<ul><li>Preparation changes timbres drastically, leading to 'dead' toneless sounds and various distortions of pitched sounds</li><li>The effect is often likened to gamelan</li><li>Textures vary from:<ul><li>Homophonic (e.g. Sonata I bar 1)</li><li>Monophonic (e.g. Sonata II bar 1)</li></ul></li></ul>

	• Two-part homorhythmic (e.g. Sonata II bar 10)
	• Layered (e.g. Sonata II bar 30)
	• Melody with pedal (e.g. Sonata III bars 1–8).
Further listening	• Cage – *Amores*.

Corelli – Trio Sonata in D, Op. 3 No 2: movement IV

Background	• Published in 1689, and therefore standing on the borderline between middle and late Baroque
	• The last movement of a four-movement sonata
	• One of a set of 12 trio sonatas
	• Although described as a trio sonata, the work requires four players: two violins, violone (the equivalent of a cello) and organ continuo
	• The organ supplies harmonies as indicated by the figured bass
	• The use of the organ has led to the piece's designation as a sonata di chiesa (church sonata), but it can be performed with any suitable continuo instrument (e.g. harpsichord), and in any performance venue.
Rhythm and metre	• In rapid compound duple time ($\frac{6}{8}$), in the style of a gigue
	• Basic motif is made up of quavers and semiquavers, with occasional longer notes in the upper parts
	• Syncopation at bars 26–27
	• Feeling of $\frac{3}{4}$ in bar 27 arising from a hemiola:
Melody	• Basic motif composed of 3rds and stepwise movement
	• Inversion at bar 20
	• Sequence at bars 8–10.
Harmony	• Functional

	• Diatonic, with chords mainly in root position and first inversion
	• Perfect cadences
	• Suspensions
	• Inverted pedals (e.g. bars 15–18, violin II).
Tonality	• D major, with modulations to related keys, e.g.:
	• A major at bar 19
	• B minor at bars 27–28
	• E minor at bars 31–32.
Structure	• Binary, with each section repeated.
Texture	• Writing for the violin is idiomatic, though Corelli tends to avoid the lowest registers and anything above third position
	• The texture is often 'polarised', i.e. two high violin parts and a low bass line
	• This movement is broadly contrapuntal with fugal elements, although the writing is also frequently homorhythmic (e.g. bars 3–4)
	• Stretto is used at bar 20, where the imitation comes after one bar only.
Further listening	• Corelli – any concerto grosso or trio sonata.

Haydn – String Quartet in E♭, Op. 33 No. 2, 'The Joke': movement IV

Background	• The string quartet was a Classical genre developed by Haydn
	• This quartet was composed in 1781, and was part of a set of six that were composed 'in a new and special manner'
	• This excerpt is the last of the four movements
	• Violin I is allocated most of the melodic interest, with remaining instruments providing support
	• The subtitle hints at Haydn's liking for wit and humour, with many of the jokes arising from the undermining of Classical conventions (e.g. prolonged dominant pedals, and unconventionally treated second inversions)
	• The work was originally intended for domestic performance.
Rhythm and metre	• The time signature is compound duple ($\frac{6}{8}$), apart from the slow (Adagio) section near the end which is simple duple ($\frac{2}{4}$)
	• Because of the speed of the music, most note lengths are generally no shorter than a quaver
	• A few demisemiquavers and semiquavers occur in the Adagio

	• Rests play an important role, especially in setting up the jokes at the end.
Melody	• Phrasing is frequently periodic, i.e. using balanced two- and four-bar phrases, characteristic of Classical-era music
	• There is much stepwise (conjunct) movement with occasional larger intervals
	• Chromatic inflections are introduced (e.g. bar 5, B♮)
	• Haydn uses occasional ornaments and appoggiaturas.
Harmony	• Haydn's harmony is functional, with frequent cadences, often preceded by the supertonic chord (as in bars 7–8):
	• Other characteristic devices include:
	• Dominant pedals
	• Dissonances such as appoggiatura chords, suspensions and the dominant 9th (bar 148).
	• Second-inversion chords are left unresolved for humorous effect (e.g. bar 47).
Tonality	• The key is E♭ major, defined by cadences and pedals
	• Modulation is limited and involves A♭ major (bar 41) and F minor (bar 49) in the first episode, with occasional brief excursions to B♭ major (e.g. bar 68).
Structure	• Rondo form
	• The opening eight bars frequently recur
	• The complete structure is:

1–36	A (1–8) B (8–28) A (with repeats)
36–70	C
71–107	A B A (no repeats)
107–140	C¹ (notice the removal of D♭s to avoid modulation)
140–148	A
148–152	Adagio
152–172	A with phrases separated by rests

Resources and texture	• A single family of instruments (strings) is used conventionally (that is, bowed throughout)
	• The main texture is melody-dominated homophony

	• Variety in texture is managed through alternations of differing numbers of parts (e.g. four parts at the opening, followed by just the three upper parts)
	 • Haydn also uses:
	   • Pedal points of both sustained notes and articulated quavers
	   • The upper two parts in 6ths
	   • Double stopping (e.g. in the Adagio).
	 • Dynamic and articulation indications are detailed.

Further listening	• Haydn – Symphony No. 26 in D minor: movement I (NAM 2) • Haydn – 'Fifths' Quartet, Op. 76 No. 2 • Haydn – Symphony No. 104 in D.

Beethoven – Septet in E♭, Op. 20: movement I

Background	• Composed in 1799 and first performed in 1800 • One of Beethoven's most conventionally Classical works • The first movement of a six-movement work • The relatively large number of movements and the size of the ensemble indicate links with the serenade type of Classical music • The size of the ensemble also makes it suitable for concert as much as chamber performance.

Rhythm and metre	• Opens with a slow (Adagio) triple time (¾) section, including demisemiquaver passages
	 • Followed by fast (Allegro con brio) duple time (₵)
	 • Rhythmic features include:
	   • Anacrusis
	   • Syncopation
	   • Triplets
	   • Diminution in the closing bars.

Melody	• The melody in the Adagio features a combination of broken chords and conjunct movement, and ornamentation (acciaccaturas and a trill)
	 • In the Allegro con brio, the opening motif of the first subject (three quavers) is derived from a similar figure in the Adagio (see bar 8, violin)
	 • Other features include:
	   • Sequence
	   • Periodic (balanced) phrasing
	   • Ornamentation (trills, acciaccaturas, turns)

	• Chromaticism • Scalic patterns.
Harmony	• Functional, with frequent cadences, both imperfect and perfect • Chords appear in root position and all inversions • The harmonic rhythm (rate of chord change) increases as cadences are approached • Pedal points are used to raise tension • There is some chromatic harmony, for example the German (augmented) 6th at bar 7.

Tonality	• The movement is in E♭ major, with modulations
	
	• Key changes are closely related to the underlying structure:
	
	  • The second subject appears in the dominant
	
	  • The development includes passages in C minor, A♭ major and F minor
	
	  • The second subject in the recapitulation remains in E♭ major.
	
	• Beethoven also touches on the tonic minor (E♭ minor) in the introduction.

Structure	• A slow introduction followed by sonata form • The main sections are:

Bars	Section
	Exposition
18	First subject
40	Transition
53	Second subject
98	Codetta
111	Development
	Recapitulation
154	First subject
188	Second subject
233	Coda

Forces and texture	• Scored for three wind instruments and four strings, including double bass
	
	• Notice the use of transposing instruments:
	
	  • Clarinet in B♭ sounds a major 2nd below the printed pitch
	
	  • Horn in E♭ sounds a major 6th below the printed pitch.
	
	• Beethoven uses multiple stops in the violin and viola for additional force
	
	• He uses many different types of texture, and constantly varies the number of instruments involved

	• The Adagio opens with a contrast between tutti chords and a single (monophonic) violin line
	
	• At bar 8, three-part string chords are heard in alternation with tutti chords
	
	• At the opening of the Allegro con brio, Beethoven uses melody-dominated homophony for three instruments, followed by an expanded melody-dominated homophony for all instruments
	
	• Other textural features include:
	
	   • Antiphony (or dialogue) at bars 47–49
	
	   • Melody in octaves (bars 111–115)
	
	   • Homorhythm (bars 53–55)
	
	   • Pedal (bars 140–153)
	
	   • Imitation (bars 258–264).

Further listening	• Beethoven – Symphony No. 1 • Schubert – Octet.

Schumann – *Kinderscenen*, Op. 15: Nos. 1, 3 and 11

Background	• Three short pieces from a set of 13 miniatures • Sometimes described as 'character' pieces, intended to convey emotional states or moods, and so programmatic to some degree (compare with Berlioz's *Harold in Italy*).

Rhythm and metre	All three are in simple duple time ($\frac{2}{4}$), but:
	
	   • No. 1 has constant triplet quavers in the accompaniment
	
	   • No. 3 has running semiquavers
	
	   • No. 11 changes tempo, and contains off-beat chords and dotted rhythms.

Melody	• All pieces are characterised by periodic/balanced phrasing and sequence • No. 1 is typified by a rising minor 6th at the start of many of the phrases:

	<ul><li>No. 3 is frequently conjunct</li><li>No. 11 contains a variety of motifs, some quite wide in range (e.g. bass line bars 9–12). There is also chromaticism.</li></ul>
Harmony	<ul><li>Functional</li><li>Particular features are as follows:<ul><li>No. 1 contains diminished 7ths and a circle of 5ths in bars 9–12</li><li>No. 3 uses a double pedal on C and G at bars 13–14, resulting in a 'Neapolitan' inflection (that is, a chord on the flattened supertonic)</li><li>No. 11 uses various cadences, including the interrupted (bar 26).</li></ul></li></ul>
Tonality	Limited or no modulation:<ul><li>No. 1 is in G major throughout</li><li>No. 3 is in B minor throughout</li><li>No. 11 is in G major, but touches on E minor and C major. Chromaticism sometimes makes statements of the key less clear.</li></ul>
Structure	<ul><li>No. 1: rounded binary with repeats</li><li>No. 3: rounded binary with repeats</li><li>No. 11: simple rondo.</li></ul>
Texture	<ul><li>Melody-dominated homophony with idiomatic piano-writing and use of the sustaining pedal</li><li>No. 3 uses a sort of 'stride' bass</li><li>No. 11 is notable for shifting the melody from the right to left hand, and for off-beat accents.</li></ul>
Further listening	<ul><li>Schumann – *Carnaval*.</li></ul>

Louis Armstrong and his Hot Five – *West End Blues*

Background	<ul><li>American trumpeter and singer Louis Armstrong was one of the most important figures in the early history of jazz</li><li>The song *West End Blues* was written by Joe 'King' Oliver and recorded in 1928</li><li>Armstrong's traditional jazz arrangement of this 12-bar blues followed just weeks later</li><li>The arrangement was not written down – the version in the Anthology is a transcription, made by notating what is heard on the recording</li></ul>

	• Improvisation is an important element in jazz. The first years of jazz favoured group improvisation, but this track is typical of the new style that emerged after 1925 in which soloists took turns to improvise over an accompaniment • The opening cadenza is famous as an example of Armstrong's virtuoso trumpet playing.

Resources	• Frontline: trumpet (Armstrong), clarinet and trombone
	• Rhythm section: piano, banjo and drums
	• Trumpet:
	   • Wide range (more than 2 octaves) and occasional use of fast vibrato, especially on long notes
	   • Pitch bend (bar 11)
	   • Lip trill on the last note (B♭) of the first chorus
	   • Third chorus features a duet in which Armstrong sings scat-style responses in counterpoint with the clarinet.
	• Clarinet: restricted to a range of a 10th in its lowest (chalumeau) register
	• Trombone:
	   • The solo is in a high register and includes numerous slides (glissandi)
	   • Elsewhere the trombone joins with the clarinet to provide sustained harmonies.
	• Piano:
	   • Stride bass (wide left-hand leaps) in solo, with elaborate right-hand part in high register
	   • Elsewhere, piano and banjo comp (accompany with steady, detached chords).
	• Drums restricted mainly to the 'bock-a-da-bock' as other percussion was difficult to record.

Structure	

Introduction	unaccompanied trumpet cadenza
Chorus 1	main theme on trumpet, accompanied by all
Chorus 2	trombone improvisation, accompanied by rhythm section
Chorus 3	improvised duet for clarinet and scat vocal, accompanied by rhythm section
Chorus 4	unaccompanied piano
Chorus 5	trumpet improvisation, accompanied by all
Short coda	piano, then all join in for the final cadence

	• Each chorus is based on the chord pattern (the 'changes') of a 12-bar blues • Improvisations are based (often very loosely) on the melody of Joe 'King' Oliver's *West End Blues*.
Rhythm and metre	• After the rhythmically free opening, most of the piece is in common time (simple quadruple metre) • Piano and banjo comp (accompany) in steady crotchets • Solos feature triplets and swung quavers: Swung quavers Written: Or: Played • Occasional use of a 'scotch snap' pattern (semiquaver – dotted quaver) • Long, sustained notes feature at the start of the final chorus • Shorter note values predominate in the piano solo and in the second half of the final chorus.
Melody	• Several broken-chord patterns and some chromatic movement in the introduction • Small leaps between chord notes, as well as occasional wide leaps, are more common than stepwise movement • Frequent use of blue notes - G♭ (often written as F♯) and D♭ in the key of E♭ major • 4-bar phrases in choruses, with phrases often linked to create flow.
Tonality and harmony	• The introduction is tonally ambiguous, but it ends on an augmented dominant chord of E♭ major. After this, the key is E♭ major throughout, with occasional blue notes and chromatic decoration but no modulation • Typical of the 12-bar blues, most chords are I, IV or V^7 in root position. A 7th is sometimes added to chord I • Occasional use of substitution chords (a common feature of jazz harmony) to provide variety – e.g. A♭ minor instead of A♭ major for chord IV, or replacing chord I with the progression II^7–V^7–I (both occur in the second chorus) • Armstrong occasionally plays away from the chord (e.g. bars 15–16, where few of the notes fit the underlying B♭^{7} chord • Some chromatic chords such as diminished 7ths – chromaticism is particularly notable in the solo piano chorus. Introduction finishes on an augmented dominant chord and the harmony at the end of each chorus is decorated with passing chromaticism

	•	The coda begins over a dominant pedal and finishes with a chromatically decorated plagal cadence. The track ends on an added 6th chord (I^6).
Texture	Introduction	the texture of the trumpet cadenza is monophonic, ending with a single homophonic chord when all the instruments enter
	First chorus	clarinet and trombone accompany trumpet (initially clarinet is in 3rds with the trumpet, later in simple counterpoint, while trombone sustains harmonies). Piano and banjo comp with steady chords
	Second chorus	melody-dominated homophony (trombone melody over homophonic chords)
	Third chorus	call and response between clarinet and scat vocal
	Fourth chorus	piano solo (melody-dominated homophony with stride bass accompaniment)
	Fifth chorus	similar texture to first chorus – starts with long-held chord for the frontline while rhythm section continues to comp
	Coda	starts with short piano solo and ends with three homophonic chords for tutti.
Further listening	•	*Muskrat Ramble* – jazz composition by Kid Ory, recorded by Louis Armstrong and his (original) Hot Five in 1926
	•	*Basin Street Blues* – song by Spencer Williams, 1926, recorded by Louis Armstrong and his Hot Five in 1928.

APPLIED MUSIC 2016

J. S. Bach – Cantata No. 48, 'Ich elender Mensch': movements I–IV

Background	• First performed on 3 October 1723, the 19th Sunday after Trinity, in Leipzig.
	• The cantata was performed before the sermon and reflected the subject matter contained in the preceding readings
	• It was intended for a small chorus and orchestra, with organ continuo
	• It is a multi-movement work which, besides chorus, recitative and aria, includes two different chorales for congregational use.

Rhythm and metre	• Movement I: triple time, with a relentless repeating pattern; includes a hemiola at bars 42–43:

	• Movement II: although notated in quadruple time, the recitative gives the impression of relatively free speech rhythms
	• Movement III: simple quadruple time
	• Movement IV: triple time ($\frac{3}{8}$), the bass line in quavers throughout, the upper parts (voice and oboe) drawing on a wider range of rhythms, e.g. the dotted rhythm of the opening phrase.
Melody	• Movement I involves a combination of:
	• The ritornello motif, with rising quavers, a plunging downward leap and an appoggiatura
	• The vocal lines, starting with upward leaps of usually a 5th or 6th
	• The cantus firmus, based on a chorale and relatively conjunct.
	• Movement II is relatively angular and characterised by a number of expressive leaps:

Bar 2	Falling diminished 7th
Bars 3–4	Rising diminished 7th
Bar 10	Rising minor 7th
Bars 14–15	Rising minor 6th

	• Movement III's melody is mainly conjunct
	• Movement IV's melody is more instrumental in nature, with demanding leaps.

Word-setting	• Movements II and III are almost totally syllabic, except for the final phrase of the chorale • Movements I and IV involve a mixture of both syllabic and melismatic underlay.
Harmony	Bach's harmony is functional, with: • Clearly defined cadences • Tierces de Picardie (e.g. movement I bar 138) • Pedal points (e.g. movement I bars 131–138, inverted tonic pedal in oboe) • Suspensions (e.g. movement I bar 34, tenor) • Some chromatic writing (especially in movement II) • Frequent diminished 7ths.

Tonality and structure	• Movement I: ritornello, but also incorporating:
	
	   • Fugato-like choral layers
	
	   • An instrumental cantus firmus (derived from the chorale in movement VII) heard in canon in trumpet and oboe.
	
	• The use of a cantus firmus (a pre-existing melody taken from a chorale) imposed severe limitations on the range of (entirely minor) keys that Bach could use, as the examples in the table below show:

Bar 1	G minor
Bar 43	D minor (though there is a tierce de Picardie at bar 44)
Bar 60	C minor
Bar 88	D minor

• The music returns to G minor with the concluding plagal cadence (bar 138)

• Movement II: through-composed recitative accompagnato (with orchestral accompaniment, as opposed to just continuo) with rapid modulations, moving from E♭ major to:

Bar 2	F minor
Bar 4	C minor
Bar 6	A♭ major
Bar 8	B♭ minor
Bar 9	Chromatic progressions and enharmonic change lead to…
Bar 11	E major
Bar 14	G minor
Bar 16	B♭ major

- Movement III: chorale, in B♭ major
- Movement IV: obbligato aria in ritornello form, in E♭ major:

1–16	Ritornello	E♭ major
16–38	Vocal solo	Modulates to B♭ major
39–48	Shortened ritornello	B♭ major
48–56	Vocal solo	C minor to A♭ major
56–60	Brief reference to ritornello	Starts in A♭ major
60–79	Vocal solo	F minor to E♭ major
1–16	Ritornello repeated	E♭ major

Resources and texture	• The cantata's use of resources is typically Baroque, with:
	
	    • Continuo providing the harmony indicated by the figured bass
	
	    • Strings
	
	    • Four-part chorus
	
	    • Vocal and instrumental soloists.
	
	• The vocal writing is demanding as a result of Bach's tendency to treat the voices instrumentally
	
	• Bach uses a wide range of textures, each movement having an individual sound
	
	• Movement I is the most complex, having three independent layers:
	
	    • String ritornello (melody-dominated homophony)
	
	    • Vocal parts (freely imitative)
	
	    • Oboes and trumpets (chorale in canon at the 4th below).
	
	• Movement II: alto with homophonic strings
	
	• Movement III: initially homophonic setting of the chorale which then becomes contrapuntal. The orchestra doubles the voices
	
	• Movement IV: walking bass with oboe solo, later on counterpoint and dialogue between alto and oboe.

Further listening	• Bach – Brandenburg Concerto No. 4 in G: movement I (NAM 1) • Bach – Cantata No. 140, *Wachet auf!*.

Schoenberg – 'Der kranke Mond' from *Pierrot Lunaire*

Background	• Arnold Schoenberg worked in Vienna, then moved to the USA in 1934. He was the leading composer of the Second Viennese School

	• *Pierrot Lunaire* (The Moon-struck Clown) is a setting of 21 poems from a cycle of poetry (translated into German) by the Belgian poet, Albert Giraud. They tell the story of a sad clown who is obsessed with, and perhaps driven mad by, the moon
	• Composed in 1912 and first performed that year in Berlin. Despite some hostility from the public towards the modernity of the music, it was well received by enthusiasts for Avant Garde music
	• Schoenberg described the work as a melodrama (speech heightened by musical accompaniment); originally it was semi-staged with the reciter in costume and the instrumentalists hidden from view
	• The musical style is atonal and dissonant
	• The work is an example of expressionism in music – the portrayal of inner feelings and psychological states, often in an exaggerated fashion
	• The vocal part uses *sprechgesang* (speech-song) in which the pitch of notes with crosses through the stem is immediately quitted by a slide (*portamento*) in an upward or downward direction
	• A flautist and reciter only are required for 'Der kranke Mond' (The Sick Moon), although the complete work requires five players (flute, clarinet, violin, cello and piano).
Structure	• Through-composed (no formal musical structure). Music responds to the imagery of the poem
	• The three stanzas of the poem are separated by short flute interludes. Each stanza is set to different and unpredictable music, to express the reciter's volatile state of mind.
Rhythm and metre	• Written in compound duple metre ($\frac{6}{8}$ time) but the slow pace and juxtaposition of a wide variety of note lengths makes it difficult to perceive a regular pulse
	• Rhythm is very flexible and influenced by the expressive portrayal of the text.
Melody	• Characterised by an unpredictable mix of semitone movement, angular leaps, abrupt changes of direction and phrases of uneven length. Not tuneful in the conventional sense of melody
	• Highly chromatic – all 12 pitches of the chromatic scale are heard before the end of bar 3, although it is not a 12-note serial piece
	• There are a few small-scale repetitions: e.g. the notes of *an Sehnsucht* are repeated for *tief erstickt*, and the vocal pitches of bar 23 are repeated for bar 24, and in augmentation for bar 25, to end the song
	• Signalling the ending, the flute part in bars 22–24 consists of a long, descending sequence.
Texture	• The thin, two-part texture (flute and voice) allows the text to be heard clearly
	• The two parts do not share any melodic material – the independent lines form a type of free counterpoint

	• The flute solos between the stanzas of the poem are monophonic in texture.
Tonality and harmony	• Atonal. No conventional chord progressions • Such 'harmony' as there is occurs when notes from the two independent melodic lines coincide.

Resources	• Reciter:
	    • Wide vocal range (nearly two octaves)
	    • Use of *sprechgesang*
	    • Mainly quiet dynamic levels.
	
	• Flute:
	    • Much of the part is in a low register
	    • Briefly rises to climactic high notes in three places.

Further listening	• Schoenberg – *Gurrelieder* (particularly the last 6 minutes) • Walton – *Façade* (particularly 'Popular Song, 'Tango-Pasodoble' and 'Scotch Rhapsody').

Bernstein – *On the Waterfront*: 'Symphonic Suite' (opening)

Background	• This excerpt is from Bernstein's only film score • It was composed in 1954, and was the underscore for a film that focused on violence and corruption in the New York docks • The score has been criticised as film music as it tends to distract from the on-screen action.

Rhythm and metre	• Opens at an *andante* tempo in simple quadruple time
	
	• The tempo increases to *presto barbaro* (bar 20), with alternating duple and triple time
	
	• Typical devices include:
	
	    • Ostinato
	    • Syncopation
	    • Off-beat accents
	    • Cross-rhythmic effects.
	
	• The final section (bar 106) is marked *adagio* and returns to quadruple time
	
	• Here long, sustained notes in the strings provide a backdrop to an isolated three-note figure.

Melody	• The opening melody spans a minor 10th • It is arch-shaped • And draws on notes from the blues scale on F minor • Minor 3rds and diminished 5ths are prominent in the opening melody, and indeed minor 3rds play an important role throughout the extract

	• The ostinato's outline is smudged by a glissando in bars 24 and 30
	• The saxophone melody at bar 42 is angular and rhythmically disjointed
	• From bar 70, this melody – now in oboes and violins – is fragmented.
Harmony	• Harmony is non-functional and frequently dissonant
	• In some passages it is difficult to hear the harmonies clearly because of the low sonorities
	• Typical tension-raising devices include:
	• Pedals
	• Tritonal clashes
	• Bitonality (e.g. G minor and D major at bar 78; B major and F major from bar 106):
	F major in two uppermost parts and bass / B major chord (E flat = enharmonic D sharp)
Tonality and structure	• Sections are strongly contrasted, reflecting different stages of the drama
	• Motivic links are created mainly through the use of minor 3rds
	• Tonality is non-functional, there being no cadences
	• The main landmarks are:

Bars	Landmark
1	Andante: opening theme in F minor (using the blues scale). Closes on F major at bar 19
20	Presto barbaro: ostinato of a minor 3rd, the basis for a layered/fugal texture. Initially in G minor, but the tonality becomes elusive with the introduction of tritones/bitonal elements
42	New theme on saxophone
54	This theme is repeated, but with shortened note lengths on woodwinds and trumpets
64	Concluding three-note figure (from bar 52) heard in simultaneous retrograde (i.e. the falling intervals of a 2nd and 6th in oboe and violin I are heard at the same time as a rising 6th and 2nd in clarinet and violin II)
78	Motif from bar 20 in tutti homophony
88	Ostinato motif and/or rhythm maintained throughout this section
106	Adagio: the three-note figure from bar 52, and its rhythm, is isolated

Resources and texture	• Large symphony orchestra with extensive percussion and solo saxophone • Wide range of textures and orchestral sonorities:

Bars	Landmark
1	Monophonic horn
7	Imitative flute and trombone
13	Two-part muted trumpets plus pedal
20	Percussion 'fugue'/riff plus sax melody
54	Theme in strings and woodwind in octaves
78	Tutti homophony
88	Sustained single note in violin plus side drum
106	Staggered build-up of chord, then sustained string chord with woodwind and brass stabs

Further listening	• Bernstein – the remaining parts of the 'Symphonic Suite' • Bernstein – 'Prologue' and 'Jet Song' from *West Side Story*.

John Williams – *ET:* 'Flying Theme'

Background	• American composer John Williams has written the music for many successful films, including *Jaws*, *Star Wars* and the first three *Harry Potter* films • Williams revived a late-romantic style of film music, using a large symphony orchestra, following a period when pop, jazz and electronic music were preferred in Hollywood movies • The music for *ET* was scored by Herbert W. Spencer, the use of a professional orchestrator being common practice in film music because of the tight schedules imposed on composers • This extract is from a concert suite based on the 1982 film score for *ET*, which is similar to the music in the film, but not identical • In the movie the 'Flying Theme' accompanies a scene in which ET (the Extra-Terrestrial) causes a bicycle and its 10 year-old rider to fly through the night sky, silhouetted against the moon.
Structure	• Rondo form (AABAB^{1}AA), with introduction and coda • The eight-bar 'flying theme' (A) is heard 5 times in the extract. The third time it is in the dominant key with transitional passages (episodes B and B^1) either side • The introduction is based on a repeating quaver figure • The coda starts with rising scales and makes reference to themes from the A and B sections.

Rhythm and metre	• The introduction and parts of the coda are in duple metre ($\frac{2}{2}$ time) but the main part of the movement is in triple metre ($\frac{3}{2}$ time)
	• Rhythms are mainly simple with little use of syncopation
	• A double-dotted rhythm at the end of the main theme is re-used in the episodes (B sections)
	• Almost continuous quavers within the accompaniment perhaps suggest gliding through the air
	• The 'flying theme' is decorated with sextuplet figures in the coda.
Melody	• The 'flying theme' is regular in structure, opens with notes based on the tonic triad (with a turn-like figure on the 3rd note) and contains wide rising leaps – all help to make the melody memorable
	• The first two bars are repeated in varied sequence
	• The entire eight-bar theme is repeated with slight changes, including a countermelody for flutes and bells
	• The episodes develop the countermelody and re-use the double-dotted figure from the main theme.
Texture	• Homorhythmic in the introduction (using a four-note ostinato) then melody-dominated homophony
	• Main melody is doubled in octaves and its wide leaps contrast with its subservient accompaniment, which consists of chords in a simple motor rhythm of repeated, 'chugging' quavers
	• Little contrapuntal interest apart from brief countermelody in bars 18–24
	• There is a little use of imitation from the horns during the last appearance of the theme.
Tonality and harmony	• Begins and ends in C major, and modulates to the dominant (G major) for the middle appearance of the main theme
	• Very traditional approach to tonality is balanced by some use of non-functional harmony, such as added major 2nds and major 7ths, and by the juxtaposition of unrelated chords in the second episode
	• The occasional use of F♯ rather than F♮ lends a touch of the Lydian mode to the key of C major
	• Some use of chromatic harmony, especially in the episodes
	• At the start of the coda, successions of parallel triads rise over a dominant pedal leading to a chord of C major underpinned by E♭s, creating simultaneous false relations. Coda ends with four bars of pure tonic harmony.
Resources	• Traditional symphony orchestra, plus piano and bells, with sparing use of other percussion
	• Almost the full orchestral forces are employed for much of the time to create a powerful orchestral sound, although trumpets are mainly reserved for the bigger climaxes

	• Pizzicato and tremolo strings are used in the second episode
	• A roll on the suspended cymbal followed by a crash from the orchestral cymbals to herald the last two returns of the main theme is an orchestral cliché but provides excitement
	• Orchestration gives prominence to the main theme, which is often doubled in octaves by upper strings, upper woodwind and (on occasion) trumpets. Piano, bassoons and the rest of the brass are used for the chordal accompaniment.
Further listening	• Jerry Goldsmith – *Planet of the Apes*: 'The Hunt' (opening), NAM 44 • James Horner – *Titanic*: 'Take her to sea, Mr Murdoch', NAM 47.

Niall Keegan (Ireland) – *Tom McElvogue's* (jig) and *New Irish Barndance* (reel)

Background	• A reel is the most popular type of social Irish folk dance. The music is in common time, with accents on the first and third beats of the bar, and features fast quaver movement
	• The jig is second in popularity only to the reel. It is a fast solo dance notated in compound time
	• Both dances typically feature two main musical ideas, each of eight bars, which are repeated and alternated to form longer structures
	• *Tom McElvogue's* (jig) was composed in 1984/5 by Niall Keegan, a player of the Irish traditional flute who comes from Newcastle-upon-Tyne in England. Tom McElvogue is a distinguished performer on the traditional Irish flute who was born and studied in Newcastle
	• The *New Irish Barndance* is a traditional reel whose origins are unknown. This version was arranged by Niall Keegan
	• Irish folk tunes are traditionally learnt by ear, and ornamented and improvised upon in performance, so there is usually no definitive version of the music. Scores are not used, and so the notation in the Anthology is a transcription, made by writing down what is heard on the recording.
Texture and resources	• The texture throughout is monophonic and the music is played on the Irish traditional flute
	• The Irish traditional flute is a wooden instrument, based on the design of the early 19th century flute. It has a conical bore (unlike the cylindrical bore of the modern flute) and lacks the complex keywork of the modern instrument
	• Total range of two octaves (from D above middle C to D above the treble stave)

	• Characteristics of performance on this type of flute include an absence of breath vibrato (but some use of finger vibrato), strong attack on lower notes, little dynamic variation, and no hard staccato. Tonguing is light and used sparingly – variety comes more from ornamentation than articulation
	• Audible foot-tapping and shouts of encouragement from the audience form part of the performance.
Rhythm and metre	• The jig is in compound duple metre (notated in ⅜ time). Most bars contain six quavers, indicating that it is a double jig (a single jig is based on crotchet–quaver patterns)
	• The reel is in simple quadruple metre (notated in ¼ time). It contains a greater variety of rhythmic patterns than the jig, including fast dotted rhythms and triplets, and short note values prevail. The tempo increases towards the end. Syncopation is introduced in bar 121
	• The metre is important in defining the type of dance.
Structure	• Both dances are in a type of binary form in which pairs of repeated sections are themselves repeated:
	• Jig: 8-bar phrases in the pattern AABBAABB (the last note forms the first note of the reel)
	• Reel: 4-bar phrases, with the first half again AABBAABB. The second half is also in this pattern, but with ever-increasing ornamentation and virtuosity.
	• In both dances there is little contrast between the A and B sections, which share some common material.
Tonality and harmony	• G major tonality – G major is an easy key for flutes that have mainly finger holes rather than keywork
	• In the jig:
	• Each A phrase ends with notes that outline a V–I perfect cadence
	• Each B phrase ends with notes that form a VII–I progression, creating a similar effect
	• Between these cadences, the leading note is sometimes flattened (to F♮), giving the music a modal/mixolydian inflection
	• There is a solitary chromatic A♭ near the end.
	• The reel includes similar, if less obvious, implied cadences and occasional chromatic notes – A♯/B♭ and C♯.
Melody	• In the jig:
	• Regular phrase structures: 8-bar sections
	• A sections always start with an upward leap of a 5th from tonic (G) to dominant (D)
	• B sections always start on the upper tonic (G).

	• In the reel:
	• Regular phrase structures: 4-bar sections
	• A sections start with an upward leap of a 6th from G to E
	• B sections start with a triadic descent from a high G
	• These features become increasingly varied as the dance develops.
	• The improvised character of the music is reflected in the constant variation of melody and rhythm.
	• Melodic figures are often re-presented in different orders – e.g. in the jig the third and fourth bars of the B section are variations of the first two bars of the A section
	• Ornamentation is important in both dances. In addition to general decoration, ornaments include a slide, mordent, acciaccatura and trill. The division of a note into three shorter notes (e.g. at the end of bar 66) is a folk-music ornament known as a treble
	• As the pace quickens in the reel, virtuosity becomes an important element in the performance.
Further listening	• *Star of the County Down* recorded by Van Morrison and The Chieftains (available on YouTube)
	• Performers from the Irish Arts Foundation (including Tom McElvogue, flute) play and talk about traditional Irish music: https://www.youtube.com/watch?v=1dUChVDsNIA.

INSTRUMENTAL MUSIC 2016

Haydn – Symphony No. 26 in D minor, 'Lamentatione': movement I

Background	• Haydn was an Austrian composer who wrote more than 100 symphonies, and was important in establishing the genre as the most significant type of orchestral music in the Classical period
	• This excerpt is the first movement of a three-movement symphony
	• It was probably composed in 1768, to be played in a concert hall by the small professional court orchestra of the Hungarian Prince Esterházy, for whom Haydn was music director
	• The nickname 'Lamentatione' ('Lamentation') refers to the inclusion of a plainsong melody associated with the suffering and death of Jesus Christ, reflecting the intention that the work would be performed in the week before Easter
	• The movement reflects the *Sturm und Drang* ('Storm and Stress') style of the early Classical period, with its minor-key opening, agitated syncopation, tense harmonies and vivid contrasts.

Rhythm and metre	• The time signature of **C** is a simple quadruple metre (four crotchet beats in a bar) and the tempo is fairly fast • Most bars feature quaver movement, sometimes provided by syncopated crotchets in the upper parts against on-beat crotchets in the bass (such as at the start of the movement). The countermelody to the second subject consists of almost continuous quavers • Wind instruments sometimes have more sustained parts • Syncopation creates a sense of urgency in the opening passage and similar sections • Short rests (e.g. at the ends of bars 8 and 16) clarify the ends of sections.
Melody	• The opening (the first subject) has two melodic strands: the syncopated upper part and the 'walking bass', heard together in counterpoint. Both feature stepwise movement and mainly small leaps • The second main melodic idea (the second subject) is the plainsong cantus firmus introduced by oboe and second violins in bar 17. Like most plainsong, it includes repeated notes and mainly conjunct movement, with only a few small leaps, while the first-violin countermelody above it is based largely on broken chords • Both melodies are diatonic – the first in D minor and the second in the relative major (F major) • The melody includes ornamentation such as trills and appoggiaturas.
Harmony	• The harmony is functional, with perfect cadences to define keys and mark the ends of sections • Chords I and $V^{(7)}$ also have an important role elsewhere, e.g. to accompany the opening bars of the second subject • Diminished 7th chords, such as in bar 13, generate harmonic tension • Dissonances created by suspensions and long appoggiaturas (e.g. E against D in bar 16) add to the harmonic tension • Harmonic sequences and a circle of 5ths progression occur in the middle section.
Tonality	• The movement is in D minor (although ends in the tonic major, D major) • The second subject is in the relative major (F) where it first appears. There are a few modal inflections in the second subject, perhaps because of its plainsong nature • The middle section continues in F major and then passes through various keys on the way to A minor (the dominant minor) • The final section returns to D minor, but this time the second subject is in the tonic major (D major).
Structure	• The movement is in sonata form (the most common structure for longer movements in the Classical period)

	• The first section (the exposition) ends at the repeat mark, and consists of the first subject in D minor followed by the second subject in F major
	• The first 16 bars (and similar passages) use periodic phrasing (balanced phrases in multiples of two and four bars) – one of the most characteristic features of the Classical style
	• In the middle section (the development), Haydn manipulates material from the first section, passing through a wider range of keys
	• The final section (the recapitulation) begins with the return of the first subject in D minor. It is followed by the second subject (now in D major) and ends with a brief coda in D major.
Resources	• This work uses a small orchestra of two oboes, bassoon, two horns and strings, typical of the early Classical period
	• First and second violins play in unison in some passages (such as the start of the movement), while violas often double the cellos (either in unison or an octave higher)
	• The cello part would also have been played by a double bass, sounding an octave below the cellos
	• The word 'cembalo' at the start of the bass part indicates that a harpsichordist may have filled out the texture by improvising chords based on the cello part
	• Oboes mainly double the violins, sometimes having a simplified version of their parts
	• The bassoon doubles the cello part, although drops out in any passages where the oboes don't play
	• Horns in D sound a minor 7th lower than written. These were 'natural' horns (without valves) and so could play only a limited selection of pitches. They are used mainly in the D-minor and D-major sections
	• The orchestral parts use a fairly modest range and none are technically very demanding.
Texture	• The orchestral doublings mentioned above result in a texture of just two-part counterpoint in the first eight bars (and similar sections)
	• This is followed by four bars of chordal (or homorhythmic) texture. The contrast is underlined by an abrupt change of dynamic from f to p, and back to f for the start of the second subject. (These abrupt changes in level are known as terraced dynamics.)
	• Elsewhere, and particularly in the plainsong sections, the texture is mainly melody-dominated homophony
	• The effect of the second violins and oboes doubling the first violins with a simplified version of the same melody creates passages of heterophonic texture.

Holborne – Pavane 'The image of melancholy' and Galliard 'Ecce quam bonum'

Background	• These pieces are examples of Elizabethan instrumental music (c. 1590s) • They feature two of the most popular dances of the time, though the complexity of the textures makes it unlikely that they were ever intended as dance music as such.
Rhythm and metre	• The Pavane has been printed in modern duple time, and draws on a range of note lengths from a semibreve down to a quaver. The longest pedal extends for six tied semibreves • The tempo is slow • The Galliard is much more lively, and is notated in $\frac{3}{2}$ • Dotted rhythms are a recurring feature • In the Galliard Holborne sometimes switches from simple triple ($\frac{3}{2}$) to compound duple ($\frac{6}{4}$) time, creating the effect of a hemiola (e.g. bar 7).

Melody	• The ranges of all parts are relatively limited
	• Holborne follows the conventions of the time:
	  • Movement is mainly conjunct
	  • Leaps are usually followed by compensating stepwise movement within the original interval.
	• Holborne also uses some inversion (e.g. bars 1–4 of the Galliard):

Harmony and tonality	• The basic harmonic vocabulary is confined to root and first-inversion chords • The Pavane is notated in D major and the Galliard in D minor • Though the harmony is not 'functional', cadences and modulation are used

	• Traces of modality persist
	• Characteristic devices include:
	• Suspensions (e.g. Pavane, bars 3–4, top part)
	• False relations (e.g. Pavane, bars 13, G♮ and G♯)
	• Tierce de Picardie (e.g. Galliard, bar 8).
Structure	• Both dances have a tripartite structure (ABC) with repetitions.
Resources and texture	• Holborne's pieces were published as being playable for any available instruments of the day, i.e. viols, violins or wind instruments
	• The instrumental writing is not yet idiomatic
	• These movements are for five parts
	• The parts are of roughly equal importance
	• Although the bass part is less rhythmically lively and includes some pedal points
	• The textures are mainly contrapuntal, with imitation and occasional inversion
	• There is some limited use of homophony in the Galliard.
Further listening	• Sweelinck – *Pavana Lachrimae* (NAM 20).

Brahms – Piano Quintet in F minor, Op. 34: movement III

Background	• In its original form, the quintet was written for strings (1862)
	• Brahms then rewrote it for piano duet (1864)
	• The third and final form – piano quintet – dates from 1865
	• The work is intended for virtuoso players
	• This movement is the scherzo and trio, the third of the four movements
	• It is in C minor, and its conclusion prepares for the return of F minor at the start of the finale.
Rhythm and metre	• The scherzo is mainly in compound duple time ($\frac{6}{8}$), though with some switches to simple duple ($\frac{2}{4}$)
	• Typical devices include:
	• Syncopation (e.g. bars 2–4, violin I)
	• Augmentation (e.g. bars 22–25, violin I)
	• Dotted rhythms.
Melody	• The melodic lines are spun out of a limited number of motifs:
	• A rising arpeggiated line (bar 2) involving a rising sequence
	• A motif opening with repeated Gs (bar 13)

- Part of this motif in augmentation forms the basis of the third idea, initially in C major:

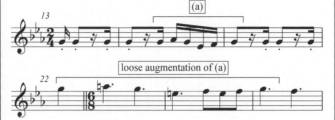

- The trio has a separate motif built partly from 3rds.
- A further typical device is fragmentation (e.g. climax of the fugato, bars 92–100).

Harmony	
	• Brahms' harmony is relatively chromatic
	• There are some modal elements (e.g. the B♭ instead of B♮ in bar 19)
	• Some characteristic harmonic features are:

Bars	Harmonic feature
1	Tonic pedal
5–6	Augmented 6th not stated vertically, but implied in the individually moving parts
19	Modal dominant chord/leading note not raised
21	Dominant chord without the 3rd
22	Diatonic, initially root-position chords
26	Secondary 7ths (e.g. V^7b of VI in C major)
39	Chordal augmented 6th, resolving to V
177	Neapolitan 6th in piano, although the B♮s in the strings from bar 178 result in an inverted augmented 6th chord
180–193	Tierce de Picardie.

Tonality and structure

- The scherzo and trio as a whole is in ternary form, involving motivic development and a wide-ranging tonal scheme
- The main landmarks are as follows:

Scherzo		
Theme	Bars	Key
A	1–12	C minor
B	13–21	C minor with modal dominant
C	22–37	C major
A^1	38–45	C minor
A^2	46–57	C minor to V of G minor

B¹	57–67	G minor, passing through B♭ minor at bar 64, D♭ major at bar 65, to V of E♭ minor at bar 67
Fugato	67–100	E♭ minor
B²	100–109	E♭ minor
C	109–124	E♭ major
A³	125–158	E♭/C minor
B³	158–193	C minor, closing in C major as a dominant preparation for the last movement
Trio		
D	193–225	C major, passing through G major at bar 203, B major at bar 209, a circle of 5ths at bars 213–219
E	225–241	V of C, with a dominant pedal
D¹	241–261	C major, with a brief reference to F major at bars 245–246

Resources and textures	• The quintet is scored for piano and string quartet (two violins, viola and cello)
	
	• Considerable demands are made on the performers:
	
	   • Piano: dense chordal textures, a wide range, single and double octaves, broken-chord accompaniment figures, and 'percussive', attacking staccato
	
	   • Strings: pizzicato, octaves for all four instruments, double-stopping and wide ranges.
	
	• Brahms uses a wide range of textures:
	
	   • A pedal plus strings in octaves at the start
	
	   • Brief imitations in the piano at bar 5
	
	   • Two string instruments in octaves at bars 13–18
	
	   • Chords plus a heterophonic line at bar 18
	
	   • String and piano chords at bars 22–29
	
	   • All strings in octaves with the piano in chordal imitation at bars 30–34
	
	   • Fugato at bar 67, later on with stretto (from bar 93)
	
	   • Piano homophony with a cello pedal at the start of the trio
	
	   • Homophonic strings with the piano playing broken chords (from bar 210).

Further listening	• Brahms – Symphony No. 1 in C minor • Brahms – *Academic Festival Overture*.

J. S. Bach – Partita No. 4 in D, BWV 828: Sarabande and Gigue

Background	• Two movements from a Suite (or Partita), which is a series of dances usually in the same key
	• Composed in 1728 (late Baroque era)
	• Intended for domestic performance on harpsichord
	• By this time, the dances were often stylised, that is the original dance elements were weakened as composers allowed their musical invention to operate freely.
Rhythm and metre	• The Sarabande is a slow, triple-time dance…
	• In which the second beat of the bar is emphasised either by length or accentuation
	• This trait is only obvious in bars 1–2, 14 and 29–30
	• Elsewhere, Bach uses less dance-like semiquaver and demisemiquaver movement
	• The gigue was traditionally in compound time, though the number of beats per bar was not firmly fixed
	• In this case, the piece is in triple time
	• There is an almost continuous semiquaver movement, with longer (dotted quaver) chords.
Melody	• In the Sarabande, the melody line is continually evolved from a basic motif
	• This process (termed *Fortspinnung*) involves:
	• Repetition
	• Sequence
	• Variation of intervals
	• Rhythmic variation.
	• The gigue opens with a broken-chord pattern
	• This then gives way to more conjunct movement
	• Occasional chromaticism features in both dances.
Harmony	• Functional, with:
	• Cadences
	• Dominant 7ths (some inverted)
	• Secondary 7ths
	• Diminished 7th
	• Neapolitan 6th
	• Suspensions.

Tonality	• Both dances are in D major, clearly defined by:
	
	   • Cadences
	
	   • Modulations to related keys, for example A major at bar 12 and E minor at bar 24 of the Sarabande.

Structure	• Binary with repeats • In both dances, the first sections finish in the dominant key, and then return to the tonic through a variety of related keys in the second section • Unusually, the second section of the Gigue is the same length as the first. In most binary form movements, the second section is longer.

Resources/
Texture
	• Written for harpsichord, so intended for an instrument with a smaller dynamic range and less sustaining power than the modern piano
	
	• The Sarabande features a variety of textures:
	
	   • Homophony (bar 1)
	
	   • Monophony (bar 2)
	
	   • Two-part, with steadily moving quaver bass supporting the more rhythmically involved upper part
	
	   • Free-voiced textures, that is a passage with varying numbers of parts (bars 11–12).
	
	• The Gigue opens fugally, that is with each part entering imitatively
	
	• The second section opens with a new melody line which becomes a countersubject to the original subject when it returns in bar 55.

Shostakovich – Prelude and Fugue in A, Op. 87 No. 7

Background	• From the late 17th century onwards, composers have written preludes and fugues as paired movements in the same key, for performance on the harpsichord, piano or organ • One of the most famous collections is the '48' by J. S. Bach (with 2 in each of the 12 major and 12 minor keys), composed in the first half of the 18th century • Dmitri Shostakovich was the most prominent composer working in Russia in the mid-20th century • In 1950 he visited Leipzig in East Germany to serve on the jury of an international piano competition to mark the 200th anniversary of Bach's death. The winner, Tatiana Nikolayeva, so impressed Shostakovich with her playing of a Bach prelude and fugue that he was inspired to write 24 of his own – a prelude and fugue in each of the 12 major and 12 minor keys

	• Shostakovich dedicated the work to Nikolayeva, and she gave its first complete public performance in Leningrad (now St Petersburg) in 1952. It had a mixed reception, with some criticism that the neoclassical style was mere pastiche – e.g. Shostakovich's A major prelude superficially reflects the A major prelude of Bach's '48' in that both are in $\frac{12}{8}$ time, largely diatonic and make frequent use of pedal points. However, Shostakovich's treatment of dissonance and tonality is totally different from that of Bach.

Structure	• A prelude is a short piece that forms an introduction to something else. Traditionally preludes for keyboard were based on a small number of motifs that recur throughout the piece, as here
	
	• Shostakovich adopts a ternary (ABA[1]) structure for this prelude, using tonality to differentiate the A major outer sections from the tonally ambiguous central section
	
	• A fugue is a composition in which a melodic idea (the subject) is introduced, imitated and developed through the interweaving of contrapuntal lines
	
	• The fugue begins with an exposition (bars 1–14), in which each part introduces a four-bar subject:
	
	    • The subject is called the answer when transposed to start on the dominant, as in the imitative entry of the middle part at bar 5
	
	    • While the middle part plays the answer, the top part continues with a countersubject. A countersubject is a melodic idea that is regularly combined with the subject
	
	    • A two-bar codetta (bars 9–10) delays the appearance of the subject in the lowest part, preventing the entries from becoming too predictably regular
	
	    • While the bottom part introduces the subject, the middle part continues with the countersubject and the top part continues with a second countersubject.
	
	• After the exposition, a fugue is less tightly defined. There are episodes (often quoting fragments of the subject and countersubject) and further entries of the subject (at least one set in a new key plus a final set in the tonic). Entries of the subject are condensed (stretto) in bars 70–72 and sustained notes resembling pedal points feature in the final bars.

Texture	• The prelude is mainly contrapuntal and much is in two parts (one in each hand, the right-hand part occasionally expanding into chords). The opening motif later swaps between the hands but there is no imitation • The fugue is contrapuntal throughout. There are three parts (three simultaneous lines), often called voices, even though the music is not sung. Like most fugues, it begins with a single line (monophony) and builds first to two parts and then three. Variety is achieved later by occasional reductions to two parts and by changes in range.

Rhythm and metre	• The prelude is in compound quadruple metre ($\frac{12}{8}$ time), with several bars in compound triple metre ($\frac{9}{8}$ time) towards the end
	• Rhythms in the prelude are mainly simple, with contrast between short note values in one hand against longer notes in the other
	• The fugue is in $\mathbf{\phi}$ time, with two minim beats per bar
	• A mix of crotchets, quavers and dotted rhythms in the subject contrasts with syncopation in the first countersubject
	• It contains near-continuous quaver movement.
	• Neither the prelude nor fugue contain many rests.
Melody	• The rhythm of the prelude's opening melody is the same as that of Bach's D major prelude from Book 2 of the '48', but the angular leaps of Shostakovich's melody are totally different
	• The semiquaver–quaver idea of this opening appears in the left hand as well as the right, and is given considerable variation (especially in the extensions of the quaver motif)
	• The melody of the fugue is entirely triadic, which results in almost all of its melodic intervals being leaps. Stepwise movement can only occur at changes of chord
	• Most intervals are 3rds, 4ths and 6ths (octaves are used sparingly). Rising movement is carefully balanced with falling movement.
Tonality and harmony	• Both movements begin and end in A major
	• Prelude:
	• The outer sections are mainly diatonic and in A major
	• Dissonance is used freely
	• The middle section (bars 13–22) is chromatic and tonally ambiguous, ending with a suggestion of the remote key of G♭ major before plunging back to A major for a return of the opening material
	• The harmonic rhythm (rate of chord change) in the prelude is variable.
	• Fugue:
	• The tonal scheme is broadly similar to the prelude, being purely diatonic in A major for the first 42 bars
	• It then shifts into F major and passes rapidly through the tonic chords of various flat keys
	• Regains A major for the final section.
	• The harmony of the fugue is very unusual:
	• Plain triads are used throughout – there is no melodic decoration, not even passing notes, and therefore no dissonance

	• The harmonic rhythm is often very slow, the same chord being used for four bars at a time, although it is faster in the codetta and episodes
	• In two-part sections, chords are implied by moving between all three notes of the triad.
	• Although Shostakovich often emphases tonic and dominant through chords and pedals, he generally avoids perfect cadences to define keys. He prefers to shift abruptly to new tonal centres rather than modulating conventionally.
Resources	• Piano: the music is of moderate difficulty and requires clear articulation, especially as the dynamic level is mainly very quiet
	• The range is of a little over five octaves, avoiding the extremes of the piano's range; in particular, very low notes are not used.
Further listening	• Shostakovich – other preludes and fugues from Op. 87, especially No.1 in C major
	• J. S. Bach – preludes and fugues from the '48', especially Book 2, No. 19 in A major.

Duke Ellington and his Orchestra – *Black and Tan Fantasy*

Background	• *Black and Tan Fantasy* was first recorded in 1927
	• Ellington was then working at the Cotton Club in New York
	• The title refers to the mixed-race nightclubs known as 'black and tan' clubs.
Rhythm and metre	• The work is in quadruple 'steady swing' time
	• Quavers are therefore uneven
	• Other features include:
	• A regular crotchet rhythm (bars 1–12)
	• A 'pad'/sustained chord from bar 13 with every other beat sounded in the bass, supporting a melody that combines duplet and triplet quavers. These are often tied across the beat with some cross-phrasing/rhythm at bar 17
	• Triplet crotchets at bar 33
	• Syncopation (e.g. bar 41)
	• Semiquavers at bar 61
	• Dotted rhythms at bar 87
	• The pulse slackens at the end.

Melody	• Pre-existing melodic material is derived from the popular song *The Holy City*, and Chopin's 'Funeral March' from Piano Sonata No. 2
	• Improvised material covers a wide range.
Harmony	• The harmony is built on a 12-bar blues progression
	• It is varied by the use of substitution chords
	• 7th/9th chords are regularly used (e.g. diminished 7th at bar 58)
	• There is a circle of 5ths (bars 59–63)
	• There are varying rates of harmonic change
	• The work ends with a plagal cadence.
Structure and tonality	• The structure is a head arrangement, consisting of:
	• A 12-bar blues with varied repeats
	• A 16-bar interruption at bar 13
	• A four-bar coda, quoting Chopin's 'Funeral March' (bar 87).
	• The piece starts in B♭ minor, changing to B♭ major for the central section that begins at bar 13
	• It returns to B♭ minor at the end, reinforced by a plagal cadence.
Resources and texture	• *Black and Tan Fantasy* requires a large group of players, involving 'reeds' (saxophones and clarinet), 'brass' (trumpet and trombone) and the 'rhythm' section (piano, banjo, drums and bass)
	• Special effects are used, associated with the 'jungle' style, e.g. growls and a horse whinny
	• Textures are predominantly homophonic
	• Specific features include:

Bars 1–12	Melody with a second supporting part, often in 6ths
Bars 13–28	Saxophone solo with more sustained supporting harmonies
Bars 29–86	Series of 12-bar improvised variations, typically with melody-dominated homophony, with one variation for piano at bars 53–64 involving stride bass
Bars 87–90	Tutti homophonic

Further listening	• Duke Ellington – *The Mooche*, *Mood Indigo* and *Creole Rhapsody*.

Miles Davis Quintet – *Four* (opening)

Background	• This excerpt is an example of bebop, a style of jazz that developed in the 1940s
	
	• Some typical features of bebop to be found here are:
	
	   • Extreme speed
	
	   • Virtuosity
	
	   • Dissonant harmony
	
	   • A small ensemble
	
	   • Chromaticism
	
	   • Fragmentation in the melody line
	
	   • Thematic substitution.

Rhythm and metre	• *Four* is notated in fast quadruple time, but feels more like duple time • It is persistently syncopated • Piano chords in the opening are frequently 'pushed', i.e. sounded just before the main beat • There is a rapid walking bass in crotchets.
Melody	• The melody is notated in E♭ major and played on the trumpet throughout • The opening material is based on a repeated, conjunct three-note figure • There is a mixture of conjunct and disjunct movement, with wide leaps more prominent in the later stages of the excerpt • There is much chromaticism • The range is wide, including a top F in the third chorus • There are numerous ornaments (e.g. fall-off at 1.15, pitch bend at 1.19, half-valving at 3.32) • The melody is fragmented (notice the frequent rests in the trumpet line of the first chorus).
Harmony	The main features are: • Dissonance • Chromaticism • 7th chords • Parallelism (e.g. bar H10) • Secondary dominants (e.g. C^7 in Chorus 1, bar 26)

	• Circle of 5ths (e.g. Chorus 1, bars 26–29)
	• Substitution chords (e.g. Chorus 1, bar 25, E♭ replaces Gm⁷).
Tonality	• E♭ major throughout, but obscured by many of the harmonic devices listed above.
Structure	• Head arrangement (a variation structure, the 'head' being the main theme) • The head consists of bars H1–16 • It is made up of four phrases (ABAB), each lasting eight bars • It is followed by a series of variations, or 'choruses' (i.e. melodic improvisations heard over the basic chords – the changes – which are also subject to variation).

Resources and texture	• The band consists of trumpet, tenor saxophone, piano, string bass and drum kit
	
	• Demands on the instrumentalists are huge:
	
	   • Virtuoso trumpet playing and improvisation
	
	   • A wide range for the trumpet
	
	   • Ornamentation (e.g. split notes, fall offs, pitch bends, ghost notes, quarter tones, half-valving)
	
	   • Rhythmic complexity
	
	   • A fast tempo.
	
	• The texture is mainly melody-dominated homophony
	
	• The sax doubles the trumpet an octave lower in the head
	
	• The piano comps
	
	• The bass plays a pizzicato walking bass.

Further listening	• Miles Davis – the CD *Milestones* • Dizzy Gillespie – *Manteca* and *A Night in Tunisia*.

> Comping simply refers to the playing of chords.

Stravinsky – *Pulcinella Suite*: 'Sinfonia', 'Gavotta' and 'Vivo'

See pages 14–16

Gabrieli – *In ecclesiis*

Background	• *In ecclesiis* was published in 1615 in *Symphoniae Sacrae*
	
	• It was probably intended for performance in San Marco (St Mark's Cathedral), Venice, where Gabrieli was organist. But it may also have been performed in other Venetian churches, notably San Rocco, where Gabrieli also worked as organist
	
	• It is a motet (i.e. a work, typically with Latin text, intended for a specific occasion or day in the church calendar, and not part of the Mass)
	
	• In its general style *In ecclesiis* mainly shows early Baroque traits, though some features are also to be found in Renaissance music
	
	• It was clearly intended for performance in one of the best-endowed churches in one of the wealthiest states of the period, as shown by the large performing forces consisting of:
	
	  • The large accompanying instrumental band
	
	  • Use of four soloists
	
	  • Choir
	
	  • Organ continuo.

Rhythm and metre	• In quadruple time ($\frac{4}{2}$) alternating with brief, dancing triple-time ($\frac{3}{2}$) sections
	
	• Towards the end there are passages, notated in $\frac{3}{1}$, with long note values to create a sense of majesty and awe
	
	• There is considerable rhythmic variety to project the sense of the text:
	
	  • Long note values (e.g. to emphasise the word 'Deus' at bar 102)
	
	  • Lively dotted rhythms (e.g. bar 32)
	
	  • Florid, rapidly moving lines (e.g. bar 68)
	
	  • Syncopation (e.g. bar 17).

Melody and word-setting	• Often stepwise, and with a relatively narrow range, even in the solo parts (e.g. first countertenor solo spans an octave, but the first baritone solo only a major 6th)
	
	• Frequent repetition of phrases (e.g. bars 3–5)
	
	• Sequence (e.g. descending at bars 13–16; ascending at bars 17–19)
	
	• Declamatory style, evident in use of:
	
	  • Syllabic style for clarity (e.g. bars 39–44, alto and tenor solo parts)
	
	  • Prolonged virtuoso melisma (bars 68 and 116–117):

Harmony	• The older, Renaissance-derived style is evident in the frequent cadences on varying degrees of the scale, use of suspensions and the consonant 4th at some cadences
	• The ending is marked by a series of perfect cadences, followed by a plagal cadence
	• The daring Baroque features include:
	• An augmented triad (bar 31, third beat with a clash between E and F):

	• Circle of 5ths, with rising 5ths instead of the more usual falling ones (bars 17–20)
	• Tertiary progressions involving unrelated chords (bar 102):

	• Unprepared 7ths (bar 104, second beat)
	• Dominant pedal to build up the tension (bars 115–117).
	• Broadly, *In ecclesiis* is in A minor, with traces of the Aeolian mode
	• Much of the motet remains close to this tonality, though the passage beginning at bar 39 touches briefly on a wider range of keys (because of the frequent use of cadences on different steps of the scale)
	• Other characteristic harmonic-tonal devices include:
	• Tierces de Picardie (often with an immediate plunge back to the tonic minor) (e.g. bar 12 beat 1)
	• False relations (e.g. bars 61–62, C♯ in cornett II, C♮ in chorus alto II).
Structure	• Refrain scheme, with variations in the instrumental and vocal forces applied (see under Forces and texture below)
	• The intervening solo sections also involve contrasting groupings
	• One of the striking features of the work is its separate instrumental section, the Sinfonia at bar 31.

| **Forces and texture** | • Besides the four vocal soloists (countertenor, alto, tenor and bass) and the chorus (alto I, alto II, tenor and bass), Gabrieli required an instrumental group of three cornetts, violin (corresponding in range to the modern viola) and two trombones. In addition there was the continuo part (basso per l'organo). |

• A range of textures is used throughout the work:

  • Monody (e.g. bars 1–5)

  • Homophony (e.g. bar 102)

  • Imitation (e.g. bars 10–11, alto 1 and tenor)

  • Canon (notably from bar 114)

  • Antiphony (e.g. bars 6–10, chorus and countertenor solo).

• The contrasting of available forces is characteristic of early-Baroque concertato style:

Bars	Forces
1–5	Vocal solo (countertenor)
6–12	Refrain (chorus and countertenor)
13–24	Vocal solo (baritone)
25–31	Refrain (chorus and baritone)
31–38	Sinfonia
39–61	Alto and tenor with instrumental group
62–68	Refrain (tenor, alto, chorus and instrumental group)
68–94	Countertenor and baritone with continuo only
95–101	Refrain (countertenor, baritone and chorus)
102–118	Tutti
119–129	Extended refrain (tutti)

| **Further listening** | • Gabrieli – *Sonata pian' e forte* (NAM 14) |
| | • Monteverdi – *Vespers*. |

Auric – *Passport to Pimlico*: 'The Siege of Burgundy'

Background	• Incidental music for one of the 'Ealing' comedies
	
	• During the 1920s, Auric was a member of *Les Six*, with Poulenc, Milhaud, Honegger, Taillefaire and Durey. They strived for simplicity, terseness and clarity, and embraced new popular styles
	
	• Auric's reputation now rests on ballet scores (some for Diaghilev) and film music, including such classics as *La belle et la bête* (Cocteau and Delannoy) and *Orphée* (Cocteau)
	
	• In this excerpt, the comic aspects of the scene are conveyed by:
	
	   • Rapid changes of thematic material
	
	   • Speedy changes of key
	
	   • Colourful and apt orchestration.

Rhythm and metre	• The material is integrated within the prevailing quadruple pulse, with only one change of time signature ($\frac{3}{2}$ at bar 51), and one significant change of tempo (*più andante* at bar 20) • Throughout much of the excerpt there is a motor rhythm of semiquavers • Rhythmic diminution is applied at bar 3.
Melody	• Two and four-bar phrases dominate • Largely diatonic with occasional chromatic alterations (e.g. bar 22) • Ornamentation (trills and grace notes) • Frequent use of scales • Relatively limited note ranges.
Harmony	Auric uses a basically functional harmonic language. The most notable features are: • Frequent perfect cadences • Added-note harmony (final cadence) • Occasional whole-tone harmony (bar 27) • Augmented 6th (bar 26) • Parallel triads (e.g. bars 47–48) and parallelism in general (e.g. in contrary motion at bar 8) • Pedals (e.g. bars 21–25) • 7th chords of various sorts (e.g. bar 58).

The 'Ealing' comedies, dating from the late 1940s and early 1950s, were so-called because of the location of the film studio where they were produced. Auric also provided scores for *The Lavender Hill Mob* (1951) and *The Titfield Thunderbolt* (1952).

Tonality	
	• Changes of key are usually sudden
	• With frequent use of tertiary relationships, the main landmarks are:

Bars	Key
1	E major
9	G major
15	B minor/major
21	E major
33	C major
39	E♭ major
43	E major
55	C major

Texture and orchestration

- The music is notated in short score with added indications regarding instrumentation
- Auric required a moderate-sized orchestra with celeste, glockenspiel and percussion
- Strings are sometimes played pizzicato
- Muted trumpet is required (bar 41)
- The bright opening has trills in the wind
- Low tremolandi are used (bar 52)
- There is considerable variety in texture, the main features being:

Bars	Texture
5	Essentially melody-dominated homophony, with the melody doubled at the 5th and octave and accompanied by parallel 3rds
9	Texture enlivened by countermelodies
15	Octaves in the bass, then dialogue between the strings and wind
21	Melody in the bass with rapidly repeated chords in the upper strings
46	Homorhythm

Further listening

- Poulenc – *Sonata for Horn, Trumpet and Trombone*: movement I (NAM 19).

Pheloung – *Morse on the Case*

Background	• The excerpt is taken from an episode in a long-running series of 'police procedural' crime dramas
	• The music is designed to be both atmospheric and unobtrusive
	• The essential effects are obtained through:
	• Limited resources (here only strings, harp, piano, four horns and oboe)
	• Limited rhythmic movement, a characteristic feature of Pheloung's style in the *Morse* music being lengthy, sustained notes
	• The slowly evolving development of a small number of motifs.
Rhythm and metre	• Though notated throughout in ⁴₄, the metre is not detectable because of the lengthy, pulseless sounds and seemingly unpredictable placing of motifs within bars
	• On paper, it is possible to see irregular diminution of motifs, although this process is difficult to identify aurally
	• A silent bar (bars 60–61) further intensifies the sense of lack of motion.
Melody	• This extract, like many other passages of incidental music in *Inspector Morse*, relies on the use of short motifs
	• The main motivic/melodic features here are:
	• Use of the Aeolian mode, except for F♯ (bar 52 and elsewhere) and A♭ (bar 92)
	• Gradual unfolding of lines built of perfect 4ths, minor 3rds and major 2nds
	• The component intervals are treated in various ways, being:
	• Inverted
	• Verticalised
	• Rhythmically diminished
	• Fragmented.

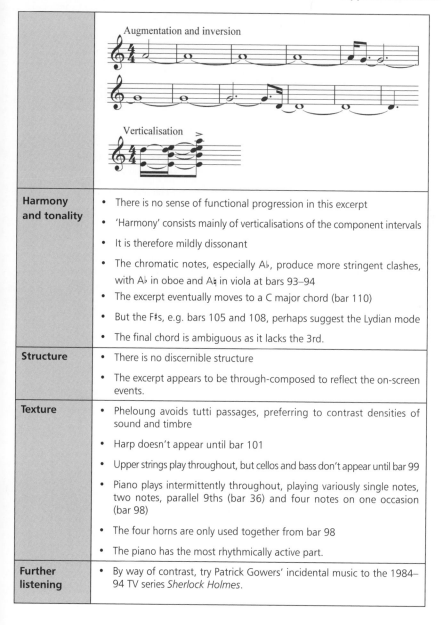

Harmony and tonality	• There is no sense of functional progression in this excerpt • 'Harmony' consists mainly of verticalisations of the component intervals • It is therefore mildly dissonant • The chromatic notes, especially A♭, produce more stringent clashes, with A♭ in oboe and A♮ in viola at bars 93–94 • The excerpt eventually moves to a C major chord (bar 110) • But the F♯s, e.g. bars 105 and 108, perhaps suggest the Lydian mode • The final chord is ambiguous as it lacks the 3rd.
Structure	• There is no discernible structure • The excerpt appears to be through-composed to reflect the on-screen events.
Texture	• Pheloung avoids tutti passages, preferring to contrast densities of sound and timbre • Harp doesn't appear until bar 101 • Upper strings play throughout, but cellos and bass don't appear until bar 99 • Piano plays intermittently throughout, playing variously single notes, two notes, parallel 9ths (bar 36) and four notes on one occasion (bar 98) • The four horns are only used together from bar 98 • The piano has the most rhythmically active part.
Further listening	• By way of contrast, try Patrick Gowers' incidental music to the 1984–94 TV series *Sherlock Holmes*.

Mustapha Tettey Addy (Ghana) – *Agbekor Dance*

Background	• *Agbekor Dance* originated with the Ewe people of Ghana
	• The version in the anthology is a transcription as the music is performed without notation
	• It was a ritual war dance, but now is performed at social events or cultural displays
	• The dance is characterised by stylised movements which symbolise the various stages of battle
	• It is played on percussion instruments only, and so the only musical aspects that are relevant here are timbre, rhythm and structure.
Instruments	There are three instruments:
	1. Gankogui – a double bell, made of iron, struck with beaters. The bells sound approximately an octave apart
	2. Atsimevu – the master drum, a relatively tall, narrow drum, played variously with one or two beaters, or else with the hand, so producing various muting effects that simulate speech rhythms. It is used to give cues to the other performers
	3. Sogo – a barrel-shaped drum, played with beaters.
Rhythm	• *Agbekor Dance* is polyrhythmic and involves cross-rhythms
	• The gankogui plays an ostinato throughout
	• This ostinato is a timeline to which the other parts relate
	• Although the time signature is $\frac{12}{8}$, the gankogui's part consists of an additive rhythm of 2+3+2+2+3 quavers, giving a syncopated effect
	• The sogo has a separate rhythm, with muting giving the impression of two pitches
	• It opens with steady, uninterrupted quavers, but eventually semiquavers and dotted rhythms are introduced
	• The atsimevu opens with steady dotted-crotchet beats, played on the wood of the drum, before introducing a wider range of rhythmic figures and groupings (e.g. semiquavers, quavers (sometimes in sets of four) and triplets)
	• At bar 21, the atsimevu doubles the ostinato.
Structure	• This element of the piece is based largely upon repetition, evolution and elaboration of basic rhythmic patterns
	• In effect it is through-composed.

INSTRUMENTAL MUSIC 2017

Berlioz – *Harold in Italy*: movement III

Background	• First performed in 1834
	• A work for solo viola and orchestra, commissioned by Nicolo Paganini, the leading virtuoso violinist of the day
	• Paganini, however, never performed it on the grounds that the solo part was not sufficiently difficult
	• This excerpt is the third movement of a four-movement symphony
	• The symphony is programmatic – it depicts a poem by Lord Byron
	• The work features the idée fixe technique already used by Berlioz in *Symphonie fantastique* (1830)
	• The idée fixe here symbolises the character of Harold and appears in all movements
	• In this movement it is heard first at bar 65 in the solo viola.
Rhythm and metre	• The movement opens with $\frac{6}{8}$ saltarello dance rhythms, with frequent dotted rhythms and stresses on the second beat of the bar:

	• The second section (bar 32) is in a slower $\frac{6}{8}$ with some bars appearing to be in $\frac{3}{4}$ (e.g. bars 37 and 38):

	• The idée fixe stands out from the rest of the texture as it is in longer notes, chiefly dotted minims
	• Unusual simultaneous presentation of all rhythmic elements occurs at bar 166
	• Augmentation is used near the end of the extract (bars 192–193).

Melody	There are several distinct melodies:
	1. Saltarello (bar 1)
	• One-bar cells, resulting in phrases of various, irregular lengths
	• Narrow range at first, later expanding to a 9th
	• Revolves around E
	• Mainly moves by step or by 3rds
	• Involves repetition, sequence and inversion
	• Modal elements hint at a folk influence
	• As do the ornaments.
	2. Serenade (bar 32)
	• Opens with a broken-chord figure
	• Phrase lengths are irregular.
	3. Idée fixe (bar 65)
	• Characteristic falling 3rd and 6th
	• Broken chords.
Harmony	• Functional, with cadences
	• Characteristic features include:
	• A double pedal (drone) in the saltarello to produce a folk-music effect
	• Secondary 7ths (e.g. bar 74)
	• Diminished 7ths (e.g. bar 41)
	• Chromaticism (e.g. bar 44).
Tonality	• C major, with only occasional modulation (e.g. G major at bars 89–90, D minor at bar 100).
Structure	Broadly a ternary form:
	• Saltarello – Allegro assai (1–31)
	• Serenade – Allegretto (32–135)
	• Saltarello – Allegro assai (136–165)
	• Coda, combining all melodic material – Allegretto (166–208).
Resources and texture	• Viola solo and symphony orchestra
	• Notice the transposing instruments:
	• Cor anglais, sounding a perfect 5th below written pitch
	• Horn in F, sounding a perfect 5th below written pitch

The absence of valve horns points to a date of composition relatively early in the 19th century.

	• Horn in E, sounding a minor 6th below written pitch.
	• Other unusual additions for this period include the harp and the piccolo (which sounds an octave higher than written pitch)
	• The texture is broadly melody-dominated homophony
	• Noteworthy devices include:
	• Drone in the saltarello section (from bar 1)
	• Divided orchestral violas
	• Octave doubling in the woodwind section (piccolo and oboe from bar 4)
	• Broken-chord accompaniment in clarinet (e.g. bars 48–52)
	• Double-stopping in solo viola (from bar 72)
	• Harp harmonics, doubling flute (from bar 167)
	• Monophonic writing for solo viola near the end (bar 202).
Further listening	• Berlioz – *Symphonie fantastique* • Berlioz – *Le carnaval romain*.

Shostakovich – String Quartet No. 8, Op. 110: movement I

Background	• Composed in 1960 following the composer's enforced membership of the Communist Party in Russia, and a visit to Dresden where it was possible still to observe the effects of bombing during World War II
	• The quartet is intensely autobiographical, with extensive use of the motif D–E♭–C–B, a musical cipher which stands for an abbreviated form of the composer's name (DSCH – Dmitri Schostakowitsch in German transliteration), as well as quotations from some of his earlier works.
Rhythm and metre	• Slow (Largo) simple quadruple time throughout
	• No values shorter than a quaver, many very much longer
	• Some dotted rhythms.
Melody	• In a low tessitura throughout
	• Melodies are often chromatic
	• Prominence is given to the DSCH motif
	• Some melodic material is taken from earlier works (e.g. Symphony No. 1 at bar 19)
	• Appoggiaturas (e.g. bar 30)
	• Conjunct movement (e.g. from bar 55)

	• Some narrow-range motifs (bars 59–60 in violin II) • Repetitive figures (bars 50–56 in the violins) • Sequence (bars 19–23 in the viola).
Harmony	• Some clearly defined, traditional progressions (e.g. a perfect cadence at bar 26, with a suspension, preceded by V–Ib–IV):

	• Less traditional chord progressions (e.g. bars 79–81 consist of G major, E♭ minor, F major, with chromatic inner parts) • There are also passages of harmonic stasis (i.e. no progression as such) e.g. the drone at bar 28, tonic pedal on C at bar 50, then dominant pedal at bar 67.
Tonality	• The tonal scheme is slow moving, starting in C minor, with a quasi-fugal answer in G minor/dominant (bar 2), and hints of F minor at bar 7 • The structure is defined partly by perfect cadences (in C minor) at bars 26, 84 and 122 • Other devices used to reinforce the tonality are the drone (on tonic and dominant) at bars 28–45 and tonic pedal at bars 50–66 • There is a major mode inflection at bar 55, a shift to A minor at bar 87, F♯ minor at bar 93, C major at bar 95, and a return to C minor at bar 105. The G♯ at the end prepares for the second movement.
Structure	The music unfolds without reference to traditional forms, though Shostakovich reprises some passages. Keys are clearly established through cadences and drones or pedals.

Bars	Section	Key
1–27	Section A, closing with DSCH	C minor
28–45	Section B	C minor (drone)
46–49	Link (using DSCH)	C minor
50–78	Section C, with reharmonisation of DSCH	C minor
79–104	Developed recapitulation of A and B	A minor (bar 87), C major (bar 95)
105–118	Based on bars 11–23	C minor
118–124	Final reference to DSCH	C minor
125–126	Link to second movement	Unison G♯

Texture	This movement for traditional string quartet exploits low tessituras throughout and draws on a variety of textures, such as:

Bars	Texture
1–11	Four-part imitation
11–13	DSCH in octaves with internal pedal in viola
19–22	Two-part counterpoint
23–27	Homophony
28–44	Drone with melody in violin I
50–78	Pedal supporting accompanying figures and melody
87–91	Chord in upper parts with melody in cello
92–94	Four-part free counterpoint

Further listening	• Shostakovich – Prelude and Fugue in A, Op. 87 No. 7 (NAM 25) • Shostakovich – Symphony No. 5, Op. 47.

Cage – *Sonatas and Interludes for Prepared Piano*: Sonatas I–III

See pages 26–28

Corelli – Trio Sonata in D, Op. 3 No. 2: movement IV

See pages 28–29

Sweelinck – *Pavana Lachrimae*

Background	• *Pavana Lachrimae* (1615) was a transcription with variations on the lute-song *Flow my tears* by John Dowland (NAM 33) • It was probably intended for performance on harpsichord, and provides evidence of the transfer of English virginalist techniques to the continent • The pavan is a relatively slow dance in three sections.
Rhythm and metre	• Notated in common time • Occasional syncopation.
Melody	• Transfer of vocal styles to keyboard with extensive conjunct movement • The descending (falling tears) line spanning a perfect 4th is sometimes changed to span a diminished 4th (e.g. C–G♯ in bars 3–4):

- There is rapid semiquaver ornamentation of the melodic material

- Use of fully notated trills

- A relatively restricted range

- Elements of the Aeolian mode, although Sweelinck frequently uses the equivalent of the modern melodic minor scale, e.g. in bars 30–31 with F♯ and G♯ ascending, and G♮ and F♮ descending

- Occasional use of sequence.

Harmony and tonality

- Sweelinck uses mainly root and first-inversion chords with frequent cadences, e.g. the Phrygian cadence as in bars 3–4 and the perfect cadences at the end of the first and third sections

- 4–3 and 7–6 suspensions are frequent:

- The pavan is in A minor with Aeolian mode inflections

- Tonality is reinforced through dominant pedals (bars 65–68 and 82–85)

- Tierces de Picardie are used, e.g. at the end of the first and last sections

- Bar 33 begins in the relative major

- There are occasional false relations (e.g. in bar 10):

Structure	• Tripartite pavan with varied repeats (AA¹BB¹CC¹).
Texture	The work has an idiomatic keyboard style, involving a range of textures:

Bars	Texture
1–4	Mainly four-part free counterpoint
5–8	Some imitation of the melody in the inner parts
9–16	Essentially chordal, with ornamental quavers passing from the inner to uppermost then inner part again
17–32	Brief imitation within the three-part texture; then running semiquavers predominate
33–39	Generally homophonic
39–41	Antiphony/dialogue between 6ths in the right hand and 3rds in the left hand
42–64	Some imitation

Further listening	• Holborne – Pavane *The image of melancholy* (NAM 13) • Dowland – *Flow my tears* (NAM 33) • Sweelinck – any set of variations.

Mozart – Piano Sonata in B♭, K. 333: movement I

Background	• The first movement of a Classical three-movement sonata • Intended as much for domestic/instructional purposes as concert use • Composed in 1783.
Rhythm and metre	• In simple quadruple (common) time • There is syncopation in the first subject, and more of a tendency for continuous semiquaver movement in the later stages of the second subject, so providing increased momentum.
Melody	• There is typically Classical periodic phrasing at the opening of the second subject

	• In contrast, the first subject consists of a four-bar phrase, answered by a six-bar passage • The movement opens diatonically, but chromatic inflections are frequent • Melodies are often extended by use of sequence • Ornamentation includes appoggiaturas (both diatonic and chromatic) and turns.
Harmony	• Functional, with cadences • Mozart uses the typically Classical cadential 6–4 • Other noteworthy features are: 　• Appoggiatura chords (e.g. bar 63) 　• Diminished 7th chords (e.g. bar 69) 　• Augmented 6th chords (e.g. bar 80):
Tonality	• Clearly defined, with modulations that delineate the structure.
Structure	The movement is in sonata form:

1–63	Exposition	
1–10	First subject	B♭ major
10–22	Transition	B♭ major
23–63	Second subject with codetta	F major
63–93	Development	Various: F major/F minor/C minor/B♭ major/G minor/ dominant preparation for…
93–165	Recapitulation (With second subject at bar 119, now in tonic rather than dominant)	B♭ major

Resources	• Early wooden-framed piano (fortepiano) with a five-octave range, as opposed to harpsichord.

Texture	• Various forms of melody-dominated homophony, with the right hand carrying the melody throughout
	• Lean textures, often consisting of only two lines, the left hand using a broken-chord accompaniment (or occasionally Alberti bass)
	• The densest chords occur at the start of the second subject (to emphasise the tonality at these points)
	• Very occasionally the right hand plays octaves.
Further listening	• Mozart – Piano Concerto No. 21 in C, K. 467.

Ram Narayan (India) – *Rag Bhairav*

Background	• *Rag Bhairav* is an example of north Indian music
	• It is similar to the chamber music of the Western classical tradition in that it is performed to a relatively small audience
	• This rag is traditionally performed in the hour immediately following sunrise
	• The term 'rag' refers to the scale and melodic content used
	• 'Tal' refers to the rhythmic pattern used.
Rhythm and metre	• The piece moves from slow, rhythmically free improvisation to music with a clear pulse and energetic rhythmic patterns
	• The rhythmically free section (the alap) extends from lines 1–13
	• The jhor (lines 14–18) is marked by a more discernible pulse
	• The jhala (line 19 onwards) is distinguished by the presence of tabla
	• The tal here is based on a tintal (16-beat) rhythmic cycle, subdivided into four vibhag of four beats each
	• Increasingly florid elaborations involve:
	• Shorter note values
	• Triplets
	• 'Irregular' groupings
	• Various types of dotted rhythm.
Melody	• Draws on a rag with a flattened second and sixth
	• Has a range of three octaves
	• Includes:
	• Improvisatory elaborations of the pakad – the underlying set of pitches that is associated with the rag being used
	• Frequent use of grace notes

	• Microtonal inflections • Slides.
Harmony and tonality	• There is properly speaking no harmony as such, only the drone provided by the tampura • Tonality is non-functional in the Western sense and there is no modulation, but tonal 'gravitation' is evident in the presence of the drone and the persistent use of the rag which homes in on C (as notated in *NAM*), with many phrases ending on C • This rag is characterised by the augmented 2nd interval.
Structure	• *Rag Bhairav* opens with the alap, a slow improvised section introducing the pakad/melodic cells (lines 1–13) • The jhor is marked by a stronger sense of pulse (lines 14–18) • The jhala (lines 19 to the end) introduces the tabla to create a strongly marked 16-beat pulse/tintal • The jhala is based on the gat (i.e. an existing composition) and is typified by an accelerating pulse, a wider melodic range and shorter note lengths.
Texture and timbre	• Essentially, *Rag Bhairav* consists of a melodic line (sarangi) with drone accompaniment (tampura) and later in the music tabla providing percussion, involving contrasting timbres • The sympathetic strings on the sarangi result in the characteristic sound of this music.
Further listening	• Any music by the famous sitar player Ravi Shankar, e.g. the CD *Ravi in Celebration* from Angel Records.

Sample questions for Sections B and C

Below are examples of the types of question normally set in these sections of the paper. Read through them carefully so that you are sure about the sort of information you are required to provide. If you are uncertain about what is meant, refer to the glossary at the end of this book.

You will notice that the examiner's commentary refers to basic points and illustrated points. A mark is awarded for a basic point without further elaboration. For example, in an essay on harmony in Holborne's pavane, a comment to the effect that Holborne uses cadences would gain a mark for a basic point. If, however, the candidate had added that there was a perfect cadence in bars 14–15, the observation about cadences would then count as an illustrated point. Very often the illustration will take the form of a location, but there may also be occasions when other types of amplification are possible. For example, in an essay on Goldsmith's score for *Planet of the Apes*, a candidate would receive a basic mark for saying that Goldsmith uses a large symphony orchestra with some unusual instruments, but an illustrated mark would be given for adding a comment about the use of ram's horn, electric harp and the like.

APPLIED MUSIC 2015 (SECTION B)

SAMPLE QUESTION 1

Describe the features of Gabrieli's *Sonata pian' e forte* that are typical of Venetian Renaissance music. (13)

Before studying the mark scheme (indicative content) that follows, attempt the question yourself. Notice that the 'key words' are 'Venetian' and 'Renaissance', so you should think about the circumstances of performance as well as the more general Renaissance features of the work. The question is open-ended; in other words, it does not specify particular features to be described. In such cases, try to comment on rhythm, melody, harmony, tonality, texture, performing forces and genre or structure. Points should be illustrated with examples from the music.

> Because you take an unmarked copy of the anthology into the exam room, your examples should normally be bar and part references where appropriate. You will gain no further credit for copying out passages of music, and will merely lose valuable time.

Indicative content	
Rhythm	• Limited variety of note lengths
	• Final part of the piece uses shorter note lengths
	• Syncopation.

Melody	• Relatively restricted range
	• Frequently conjunct, the largest interval being an octave, with 4ths and 5ths occurring more frequently.
Harmony	• Root-position and first-inversion chords dominate, with an occasional consonant 4th
	• Cadences include perfect, imperfect (Phrygian) and plagal
	• Tierces de Picardie
	• Various suspensions.
Tonality	Dorian mode on G. Cadences on various degrees of the mode producing a 'wandering' tonality.
Texture	Polychoral; antiphonal; mainly contrapuntal, with some occasional homophony; imitation.
Resources	• Uses typical Renaissance instruments – cornett, old violin (with a range similar to the modern viola) and trombones (or sackbuts)
	• Writing is not yet idiomatic, the music showing signs of 'vocal' styles.
Structure	Through-composed, so revealing links with sacred vocal works (e.g. motet).
Context	Designed for performance in St Mark's Basilica, Venice, thus allowing use of spatially separated galleries, in this case involving two four-part groups.

As previously mentioned, examiners arrive at a final mark for these questions using a holistic grid. For full details see Edexcel's *Sample Assessment Materials*. For the present, it is enough to know that the full 13 marks will be awarded to work which contains at least nine relevant, well-illustrated points, showing excellent organisation and planning, and expressed coherently without significant spelling or grammatical errors.

As you work through this section of the book, and see examples of work of different standards, you will see how the holistic grid is applied across the available mark range.

Sample answer 1

Gabrieli's work stands on the borderlines of Renaissance and Baroque music. Some works, such as the motet *In ecclesiis*, show definite signs of the Baroque with the use of continuo instruments and the combination of voices and instruments. In contrast, *Sonata pian' e forte* is quite old-fashioned and in many ways shows stylistic traits of the Renaissance era.

A good opening paragraph, establishing the historical context.

This is immediately apparent in the instrumental writing. Although Gabrieli specified particular instruments, such as violin, cornett and trombones, his writing for them is not idiomatic, and in fact looks more as though it derives from vocal models [1], especially the sacred music of the 16th century. This in itself has an influence on the nature of the melodic writing. Stepwise writing is frequent [1], and leaps are rarely more than a 4th or 5th [1].

Harmony and tonality also contain aspects that point towards the Renaissance. The work is modal, being written in the Dorian mode on G [1]. Gabrieli cadences on most steps of the Dorian scale, leading to a fluid tonal scheme, for example G at bar 25, C at bar 31, B♭ at bar 43 and D at bar 54 [1 – illustrated point]. Cadences include perfect (e.g. bar 25), Phrygian (bars 16–17) and plagal at the end [3 – locations given]. As often happens in music of this period, a tierce de Picardie is frequently used at the end of sections, and also at the end of the work [1 – location given].

Texture is also typically Renaissance. Often the music is contrapuntal [1], and from bar 71, there is a series of close imitations [1 – location given] in most of the eight parts, contributing to much of the excitement in the closing stages of the work.

The characteristically Venetian aspects of the music come with the division of the eight parts into two groups of four instruments. These would have been placed in separate galleries in St Mark's, Venice [1], where Gabrieli was organist and director of music. It allows him scope for striking antiphonal exchanges [1] and grandiose tuttis.

Overall, the work is highly typical both of Venetian methods of the times and older Renaissance music in general.

Examiner's points

This was a very good answer with 13 observations, many of which were well-substantiated. It was coherent and well-expressed, and would have been awarded full marks. Notice that not all observations can usefully be supported by examples, for example the general point that the work is in the Dorian mode in G. There is indeed little point in giving examples of features which occur throughout, such as stepwise movement.

Exercise

List further features that the candidate could have included.

Sample answer 2

Mark this answer yourself, commenting at the end on its good points, but also mentioning ways in which it could have been improved. After completing your marking, check your assessment against the examiner's points below.

> *Sonata pian' e forte* shows many features of Renaissance music. It is modal as it is in the Dorian mode, transposed to G, and the harmony is characterised by almost constant use of Picardy thirds, e.g. at the end.
>
> Textures are clearly Renaissance in style, being mainly contrapuntal. Much of this counterpoint is free, with the parts independent of each other, but Gabrieli also uses some imitation, particularly near the end.
>
> Rhythms are typical of this period as they are rather simple, though again at bar 71 things become more complicated, and there is even some syncopation (in the cornett).
>
> An important feature of *Sonata pian' e forte* is the use of antiphony. This often occurs in Venetian music as the building the music was meant to be played in — St Mark's — has widely-spaced galleries for musicians. This was ideal for playing off different groups against each other.

Examiner's points

The credit-worthy points are as follows:

➤   Modal, Dorian in G

➤   Tierce de Picardie (location given)

➤   Contrapuntal

➤   Imitation (but the location was insufficiently precise for credit)

➤   Basic rhythms

➤   Syncopation at bar 71 (location given)

➤   Antiphony

➤   St Mark's galleries.

The total was eight points, not all illustrated when possible. Such a response is regarded as 'competent'. The writing was coherent, though it would have been possible to deal with textural features (counterpoint and antiphony) together. Clearly, very much more could have been included. The final mark would be **8/13**.

Exercise

List additional points that the candidate could have made. Provide a final 'summarising' sentence to round off the answer.

SAMPLE QUESTION 2

Identify rhythmic and melodic features of *Baris Melampahan* that indicate that it is an example of gamelan music. (13)

Before studying the mark scheme (indicative content) that follows, attempt the question yourself. Notice that the key words are 'rhythm', 'melody' and 'gamelan'. You may find it convenient to refer briefly to the work's context, but take care to keep your remarks relevant. Do not waste time on any aspect of *Baris Melampahan* that is not to do with rhythm and melody.

Indicative content	
Rhythm	• Regular pulse throughout
	• Until the slowing down at the end of the extract
	• Constant on-beat pulse
	• With some off-beat sounds from the reyong and kendhang
	• Rhythms are occasionally displaced
	• Organised in rhythmic cycles – gongans
	• Consisting of four ketegs
	• Each keteg lasts four beats
	• Gongs mark the end of each cycle.
Melody	• Based on a 'nuclear' melody
	• Involving pitch numbers 1, 2, 3, 5 and 6 from the pelog scale
	• This pentatonic version of the scale is known as the pelog selisir
	• Difficult to describe component intervals because of the tuning that differs from e.g. European tuning
	• Frequent repetitions
	• Heard in varying degrees of completion
	• The only significant departure occurs at [H], the 'high tune'.

Sample answer 1

Rhythm
- *Gongs mark divisions between the cycles* [1]
- *The cycles are called gongans* [1]
- *They consist of four ketegs* [1]
- *Ombak effects.*

Melody
- Nuclear melody [1]
- Treated heterophonically
- Alternates with angsel and kendhang [1]
- Based on five pitches – selisir pelog [1].

Examiner's points

The candidate made six basic points in a rather sketchy way. At most, the answer would gain **7/13**.

> ### Exercise
>
> Rewrite the candidate's statements in continuous prose to remove ambiguity.

Sample answer 2

Mark this answer yourself, commenting at the end on its good points, but also mentioning ways in which it could have been improved. After completing your marking, check your assessment against the examiner's points below.

The war-like qualities of this piece, played by a group based right in the central region of Bali, are conveyed by the insistent rhythms, maintained until the very end of the extract where there is a slowing down. The music has a distinct four-beat feel, and each rhythmic cycle (gongan) consists of four four-beat bars or ketegs.

The overall impression is quite different from western music as the instruments are tuned differently. In fact tuning varies from region to region, and the impression is further complicated by the fact that the metallophones are often slightly out of tune with each other, producing the ombak effect.

Gamelan music is based on the pelog scale. This consists of seven notes, but in this case the music draws on only five pitches (C♯, D, E, G♯, A) as given in the preface in the anthology, though these pitches are only very approximate. At some points, the music moves into a higher pitch region ('the high tune'), but the group sticks to the same basic pitches, an octave higher.

The tune is initially heard on the ugal, the largest of the two-octave metallophones, and later is heard decorated on the gangsa, sangsih and polos, producing the heterophonic effect which is so characteristic of gamelan music. The basic four-bar phrase is often repeated, producing the characteristic hypnotic effect of this music.

This is communal music, and the whole village takes part in the performance.

Examiner's points

Credit would be awarded for mention of:

➢ Insistent rhythms

➢ Slowing down at end of the piece (location given)

➢ Gongans

➢ Ketegs

➢ Four four-beat cycles

➢ Tuning

➢ Five-note scale

➢ Higher pitches

➢ Repetition.

There are nine points with little illustration. It was well-written, but marred by some irrelevance. It would gain **10/13**.

Exercise

Draw up revision notes for this piece on texture, timbre, structure and circumstances of performance.

INSTRUMENTAL MUSIC 2015 (SECTION C)

SAMPLE QUESTION 1

Compare and contrast the approach to texture in the three pieces listed below. (36)

➢ **Cage – *Sonatas and Interludes for Prepared Piano*: Sonatas I–III (NAM 10)**

➢ **Beethoven – Septet in E♭ Major, Op. 20: movement I (NAM 17)**

➢ **Schumann – *Kinderscenen* Nos. 1, 3 and 11 (NAM 23)**

Before studying the mark scheme (indicative content) which follows, attempt the question yourself. Notice that the key word is 'texture'. You may find it convenient to refer briefly to the context of each work, but take care to keep your remarks relevant. Do not waste time on any aspect of the listed works which does not concern texture.

Indicative content

Points should be illustrated with examples from the music.

Cage	Textures include:
	• Homophonic
	• Monophonic
	• Two-part homorhythmic
	• Layered
	• Texture closely linked to timbre of prepared piano
	• Some 'dead' sounds
	• Gamelan qualities.
Beethoven	• Chords for varying numbers of parts
	• Monophony
	• Antiphonal exchange/dialogue
	• Melody-dominated homophony
	• Some broken chord accompaniment
	• Some syncopated inner parts
	• Octaves
	• Thematic combination.

Schumann	No 1:	• Mainly in three parts
		• Melody + accompaniment with broken chords in middle
		• Detached quavers in bass masked by pedal
		• 3rds in RH at bar 9 in counterpoint with bass.
	No 3:	• Leaping/stride LH with mainly single-line melody
		• More sustained writing from bar 13 leading to longer chord at bar 15
		• With ascending scale in middle part.
	No 11:	• Three-part, broadening to four parts
		• Bass melody with off-beat RH chords
		• Chords for all parts.

Sample answer 1

The works are dealt with in chronological order.

    Beethoven disliked the Septet, apparently, because it seemed to him to be too Classical. It is an outstanding example of this style, being fundamentally homophonic in texture [1]. Having said that, he obtained considerable variety within the work, partly by varying the number of players performing at any one time, and also by changing the type of texture used. ←

Avoid underlinings in continuous prose.

1   Tutti chords [1]

2   Monophonic violin [1]

8   Chords in three parts for strings [1]

19   Three-part strings melody-dominated homophony [1] with broken-chord figure in viola

Avoid abbreviations in continuous prose writing.

29   Tutti mdh, with syncopated inner parts [1] ←

40   Monophonic solo violin ←

This type of texture has already been credited.

47   Antiphonal exchange between wind instruments, answered by strings [1]

86   Three-part string chords ←

This has already been credited.

111   Mainly octaves [1] ←

Accept.

Schumann only had a piano for this piece, so the range of textures won't be so large.

No. 1: 3-part mdh, with broken chord in middle part [1]

No 3: Oom-pah LH [1] ←

Accept.

No 11: Mdh, but here LH has tune sometimes (bar 9) [1]

Cage was also writing for a single piano, but had a much wider range of sounds and timbres because of the preparation [1] which changed the effect, e.g. the occasional clunks and twangs. Some of the basic types of texture are as follows:

Sonata 1: chordal [1], pretty well throughout, but see last line for basic chords.

Cluster chords at bar 10 [1]

Sonata II: single line at start [1] building up to 3 layers at bar 30, with longest notes in bass [1]

Sonata III: Closest to mdh at bar 19, with melody in RH [1] None of these pieces has much in the way of counterpoint. ←

Accept.

Examiner's points

17 points were made, with some illustrated. Unfortunately, the mark will have to be adjusted because of the wrong format and use of underlinings and abbreviations, none of which should appear in a passage of continuous prose. A mark of 22/36 is appropriate.

> **Exercise**
>
> Rewrite the paragraph on Schumann in continuous prose, expanding on the points already made.

Sample answer 2

Of the three works, the most modern is the Cage, and this is the one with the thickest textures. The preparation of the piano results in a dense, percussive sound. It is sometimes compared to a one-man percussion band and certainly sounds rather like a gamelan. The effects are obtained by putting bits and pieces between the strings to alter the timbre. The first sonata is typified by its use of chords [1]. The first is a G^7, and so sounds quite dissonant, but not as dissonant as the really thick cluster chords in bar 10 [1]. The last type of chord comes in bars 20 to the end, where both hands are in the treble clef.

Unhelpful expression, best avoided.

Not enough for a mark.

There are not so many chords in Sonatas II and III, making this music more contrapuntal [X]. There are also a number of trills and flourishes to hold our interest. Another interesting texture effect comes from the pedals.

This remark is unclear.

The earliest piece is the Beethoven Septet. Because there are seven players here, Beethoven could produce some really thick sounds, especially when the strings players double stopped. At times he has all the players at once (tutti), like the chord at the beginning [1]. This is followed straight away with a single violin playing monotony.

An unfortunate use of an incorrect term!

It goes on like this throughout. Often there are only three players at one time, e.g. bar 19 where the strings have the main theme. Here there are single bass notes and a sort of Alberti bass in the viola [1].

The remark has been accepted, although properly speaking the viola plays broken-chord figures as opposed to a true Alberti pattern.

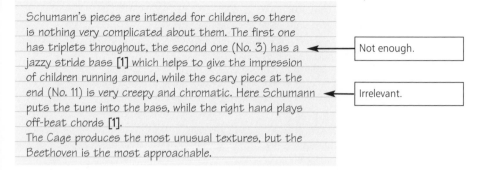

Schumann's pieces are intended for children, so there
is nothing very complicated about them. The first one
has triplets throughout, the second one (No. 3) has a   ← Not enough.
jazzy stride bass [1] which helps to give the impression
of children running around, while the scary piece at the
end (No. 11) is very creepy and chromatic. Here Schumann   ← Irrelevant.
puts the tune into the bass, while the right hand plays
off-beat chords [1].
The Cage produces the most unusual textures, but the
Beethoven is the most approachable.

Examiner's points

There are six points, some of which are appropriately illustrated. There is also
irrelevance and misuse of terminology. There is little evidence of planning. This work
comes into the 'basic' category, with a mark of 15/36.

Exercise

Correct the errors, and expand the remarks on the Beethoven Septet.

Sample answer 3

Mark this answer yourself, commenting at the end on its good points, but also
mentioning ways in which it could have been improved. Check your assessment
against the examiner's points which follow after completing your marking.

The most varied textures are to be found in the
Beethoven. This is scarcely surprising as the other two
pieces are for piano. Admittedly Cage prepared the piano,
inserting all manner of objects into the inside of the
piano, and this increased the range of sounds available
to him. Some obvious textures in the Cage are the chords
in Sonata I and the single-line writing in Sonata II (see
opening). He also uses two parts together with the
same rhythms, and in Sonata III there is use of ostinato
accompanying the melody. With Cage, everything is
subservient to the rhythmic schemes, or fractal patterns.
Unfortunately these are inaudible, and the preparation
makes it difficult to talk about what you can hear.

Working backwards, the Schumann uses melody-dominated homophony throughout. In the case of the first piece, he writes a typically romantic texture, with the melody in the top part, accompanied by triplet broken chords in the middle and supported by quavers in the bass, sustained by way of the pedal. At one point the top part is doubled in 3rds, and is heard in a sort of counterpoint with the bass.

Hasche-Mann has a stride bass accompaniment, with low bass alternating with a higher chord. The most varied textures come in the final piece Fürchtenmachen, which opens with a melody line in the right hand with a rhythmically independent accompaniment from the left hand. At bar 5, Schumann reverses the roles, with the previous melody placed in the left hand. He carries on with this method at bar 9, but here the melody is accompanied with off-beat right-hand chords. Very briefly, Schumann also uses block chords (bar 24).

Beethoven's Septet opens with a chord for all seven instruments, answered by monophonic violin. The introduction also uses homophony for three instruments, and later on the violin is given a rhythmically independent melody line. The first subject of the sonata form proper is given to three instruments in a melody-dominated homophonic texture. The melody is given to the violin, supported by the viola with broken chords and the cello providing intermittent crotchets. When this theme is repeated at bar 29, the clarinet takes the melody, supported by sustained notes on the other wind instruments and syncopations in the upper strings and a steady crotchet figure in the cello. Another textural device is a form of antiphony or dialogue between the wind and strings at bar 47, and Beethoven also uses most of the instruments in octaves at the start of the development.

Of the three works, Beethoven's is the most interesting. He achieves more contrast than can be found in the other works, partly by varying the number of instruments in play as well as changing the textural layout rapidly.

Examiner's points

Credit was awarded for:

➢ Preparation of piano

➢ Chords in Sonata I

➢ Single line

➢ Two-part with same rhythm

➢ Ostinato with melody (allowed, thought the use of the term ostinato is a little dubious)

➢ Melody-dominated homophony in Schumann

➢ Implied three parts in No. 1

➢ Broken-chord middle part

➢ Bass part

➢ Upper part in 3rds with bass counterpoint

➢ Stride bass

➢ Reversal of left- and right-hand roles

➢ Off-beat chords

➢ Block chords

➢ Tutti chord in Beethoven

➢ Monophonic line

➢ Three-part chords

➢ Description of texture at bar 19

➢ Description of texture at bar 29

➢ Antiphonal exchange

➢ Octaves.

There were 21 valid points, many well illustrated. The essay was well-written and had some sort of plan in that it worked backwards chronologically, keeping the Beethoven to the end. There was a little irrelevance, but this work would be placed in the top category with 32/36.

Exercise

Using your study guides and any other sources you have, draw up revision notes for all the instrumental works for 2015, making sure you are equipped to write on rhythm, metre, melody, harmony, tonality, structure, texture and general context and circumstances of performance.

SAMPLE QUESTION 2

Compare and contrast the approach to structure and tonality in the three pieces listed below. (36)

➢   Corelli – Trio Sonata in D, Op. 3 No. 2: movement IV (NAM 15)

➢   Haydn – String Quartet in E♭, Op. 33 No. 2: movement IV (NAM 16)

➢   *West End Blues* (NAM 48) as recorded by Louis Armstrong and his Hot Five

Before studying the mark scheme (indicative content) which follows, attempt the question yourself. Notice that the key words are 'structure' (i.e. form) and 'tonality' (i.e. keys and modulation). You may find it convenient to refer briefly to the context of each work, but take care to keep your remarks relevant. Do not waste time on any aspect of the listed works which do not concern structure and tonality.

Indicative content
Points should be illustrated with examples from the music.

Corelli	• Binary form with repeated sections • Monothematic • Main theme treated imitatively (fugally) • In inversion • In stretto • Functional tonality • With cadences • Pedal points • And modulation to closely related keys • First section closes in dominant • Second section cadences in relative minor, E minor and G major.
Haydn	• Rondo form • Functional tonality • With cadences • Pedals • But very few modulations • E.g. A♭ from bar 36 • F minor from bar 48 • Humorous 'mistreatment' of second-inversion chords at cadences.
Armstrong	• Twelve-bar head with choruses/variations • Free introduction touching on C minor, B♭ minor • 12-bar sections in E♭ throughout • Modified plagal cadence at close.

Sample answer 1

The structures of these pieces are all radically different and to some extent reflect the historical periods in which they were composed. The Corelli is in binary form [1], with the first section from bars 1–19 repeated [1], as is the rest of the piece. It is based on much the same material throughout [1], so the opening idea is immediately imitated in fugal style by the second violin [1], and is later heard inverted at bar 20 [1], where it is also heard in stretto, the second violin coming in after only one bar as opposed to two [1].

Accept as a non-technical way of saying monothematic.

In contrast, the Haydn movement is in rondo form [1], which means its main theme keeps coming back, separated by episodic material. The main theme, heard in bars 1–8, returns at bar 28, then at bars 71, 99 and 141 [1 further mark].

West End Blues is a 12-bar blues [1], with a six-bar introduction [1], then the Head, which forms the basis for variations [1] for trombone, clarinet and scat voice, piano and finally the complete group. The 12-bar cycle is kept going right the way through the piece without change.

A somewhat misleading statement as the final version is slightly extended. In other variations, there are harmonic changes which mask the basic harmonic progression.

In some ways, these pieces have more in common with regard to tonality as they all use functional harmony and cadences [1] to define the key, though the odd thing is that the earliest piece is the one which modulates the most [1]. The first section opens in D and at the double bar moves to the dominant, A major [1] with a perfect cadence [1]. In the second part of the piece, Corelli cadences in B minor at bars 27–28 [1], emphasised by the hemiola, a very characteristic device of the period. It then goes on to touch on a variety of other keys before closing in D.

True, but irrelevant.

There is not enough detail for a mark here.

Haydn, as already stated, does not modulate as much. Most of the time he stays in E♭ [1], emphasised by constantly repeated cadences, especially at the end [1] as part of the 'joke', and long dominant pedals [1]. In marked contrast, however, he introduces unstable keys at bar 36 where he goes to A♭ [1], but does not resolve the cadential second inversion in the conventional way [1].

The least stable part of West End Blues is the introduction which hints at C minor before the pause [1]. In contrast, the main part of the piece does not move from E♭ at all [1].

Examiner's points

The candidate made 22 points altogether, some of which were well illustrated. The layout was perhaps a little clumsy, and little is gained by considering structure and tonality separately as structure is often defined by handling of keys. There were one or two irrelevant or misleading statements, but overall this essay would come into the 'excellent' category and gain 31/36.

Sample answer 2

Corelli's Sonata is in binary form [1] and has an interesting tonal scheme with the high violins and low bass producing a polarised texture, so producing some striking tone colours, further enhanced by the twang of the harpsichord. Both parts are repeated here [1]. This is in marked contrast to *West End Blues* where there are no repetitions at all. It goes straight through without stopping, but is divided into sections which clearly have different tone colours. It is more interesting than the Haydn and the Corelli which are only for strings. Armstrong uses trumpet, clarinet and trombone, as well as piano and bass. He even introduces a milk-bottle rhythm (boca-di-boc) and most unusually he uses scat. This is the wordless singing effect, heard here in call-and-response to the clarinet. There are lots of interesting sound effects as a result to keep the listener's interest.

Haydn did what he could with the instruments he had at his disposal. The piece is in rondo form [1], with frequent returns of the main theme. He could have done more to vary this theme, but at least at the end he split it up into a series of short phrases which make it difficult to tell when it finished.

West End Blues is a 12-bar blues [1].

> The candidate has misunderstood tonality.

Examiner's points

There are four points here, with no illustration of devices. The question has been misunderstood in significant measure, and there is no sign of effective planning. It would come in the 'limited' category, and be awarded 10/36.

Sample answer 3

Mark this answer yourself, commenting at the end on its good points, but also mentioning ways in which it could have been improved. Check your assessment against the examiner's points which follow after completing your marking.

Corelli was a mid-Baroque composer, and it is possible to see in his work the workings of the recently invented tonal system, using major-minor keys as opposed to varieties of modal scales. He was an Italian composer who specialised in the writing of concerti grossi as well as trio sonatas, and liked to put on concerts involving large numbers of string players. In spite of this, it is best to perform his work with one player a line, in this case two violins, a bass and the harpsichord to play the harmonies.

Corelli's approach to tonality depends on functional cadential progressions and modulation to related keys. In fact, movement through the keys helps to underline the structure. Like many Baroque composers, he often wrote in binary form (see Bach's suites and partitas), and this is no exception. The key scheme, as stated above, is linked to the structure. The first part ends at bar 19 with a modulation to A major, the dominant. As was customary, in the second part of the movement (from bar 20 to the end), Corelli went through more keys, touching on B minor, the relative minor by bar 28, and then G major at bar 31 and D major at bar 35. Notice also the interrupted cadence at bar 41 before the final phrase brings us home in the last bar.

Haydn also modulates extensively, moving to the dominant Ab at bar 17. Later he touches on F minor (bar 48) before returning to the tonic. He frequently uses pedals, both tonic and dominant, e.g. the tonic pedal on Eb at bar 36. This movement is in rondo form.

The key of *West End Blues* is also Eb, and unlike the earlier pieces, Armstrong keeps in this key throughout. It is a 12-bar blues which means it has a fixed harmonic progression based on chords I, IV and V, varied by occasional substitution chords which can result in circles of fifths. It hints at different keys in the introduction, notably C minor and Bb minor at bar 4 (with the Gb and Db). Another interesting effect comes at the end with the added sixth chord, preceded by a decorated plagal cadence.

Examiner's points

The credit-worthy points are as follows:

➢   Major-minor tonal system (i.e. functional)

➢   Cadential progressions

➢   Modulation to related keys

➢   Binary form

➢   A major, dominant

➢   B minor at bar 28

➢   F minor at bar 48

➢   Pedals

➢   Rondo

➢   Accept Armstrong staying in E♭ throughout

➢   12-bar blues

➢   Different keys in introduction

➢   Decorated plagal cadence.

Notice that marks were not awarded for the incorrect key analysis, descriptions of pedals in the Haydn and the circle of 5ths in Armstrong.

Though well-written in general, there was an over-extended introduction which was tending to irrelevance, and the candidate failed to round the essay off. The work would count as 'competent', and be awarded 23/36.

Exercise

Prune the introduction and provide a conclusion.

APPLIED MUSIC 2016 (SECTION B)

SAMPLE QUESTION 1

'Disturbed' and 'disoriented' are expressions which have been used to describe Schoenberg's *Pierrot Lunaire*. Describe elements of 'Der kranke Mond' (NAM 40) which support such a view. (13)

Before studying the mark scheme (indicative content) which follows, attempt the question yourself. Notice that the key words are 'disturbed' and 'disoriented'. This question is also open-ended, so try to comment on such aspects as rhythm and metre, melody, harmony, tonality, texture, and performance forces.

Indicative content

Points should be illustrated with examples from the music.

Subject matter	One of a series of poems by Giraud concerning a moonstruck clown.
Tonality	• Atonal • Chromatic.
Texture	Lean single line accompaniment/absence of harmonic support.
Melodic style	• Angular • Irregular phrasing.
Rhythm	Irregular patterns make pulse difficult to discern.
Techniques	Sprechgesang/pitches not clearly focused.
Structure	• Through-composed • Verse refrains ignored in musical setting.

Sample answer 1

Schoenberg, a leading exponent of Expressionism in the years immediately preceding the First World War, remarked of *Pierrot Lunaire* that it was written in an ironic and satirical vein. In fact, with subject-matter based on a clown whose sanity is in doubt [1], it has become an almost classic example of 'disoriented' and 'disturbed'. It is not difficult to see how this has come about. The work is highly chromatic [1] and brings in all 12 pitches of the chromatic scale within the first few bars. It is so chromatic that it is mainly atonal [1]. Structure is another area where the disturbed nature of the poem is shown. The poem has a refrain, but Schoenberg deliberately avoided using it, and his setting is through-composed [1], without any repetitions at all. The pulse is difficult to make out [1]. There are occasional silences [1], and the melody is full of large awkward leaps [1].

The singer has to use sprechgesang [1], and the off-centre pitches also have a disruptive feel to them. Another destabilising effect comes with the thin accompaniment — just a single flute — and the absence of harmony [1].

Pierrot Lunaire was an epoch-making work that came to be regarded as an archetypal example of this composer and the period in which he worked.

> This is misleading, as there is repetition in the vocal line in bars 23–25, the last repetition involving rhythmic augmentation.

> Point accepted.

Examiner's points

The candidate made nine relevant points, with limited illustration. This work is basically well-written and shows some sense of the historical context. It would be awarded 9/13 ('confident').

Exercise

The candidate could have improved on the mark by illustrating the points about pulse and an angular melody line. List examples of irregular rhythmic patterns and large intervals.

Sample answer 2

Schoenberg was a pioneering composer whose work was atonal [1]. He invented serialism, which meant the use of 12-note tone-rows, i.e. all 12 pitches used one after another. These rows can then be inverted, retrograded or both together. All 12 notes are used in the first three bars of NAM 40, so showing a serialist approach.

Schoenberg's music is not easy-listening, and this is hardly surprising as the subject matter is about derangement [1]. The whole work is about a clown teetering on the brink of insanity, and if he wasn't feeling disoriented and disturbed to begin with, he certainly was by the time Schoenberg had finished with him! He writes the oddest stuff here. Unlike say the Bach cantata, which has solid harmonies supporting the voices, all Schoenberg uses is a single flute [1]. This must have made it very difficult for the singer to keep in tune, and what makes it even worse are the horribly difficult melody lines with huge leaps [1] and awkward chromatic passages [1], e.g. the serial passage at the start [X].

In the end, it probably does not matter that much if the singer is a bit off-pitch as it can add to the atmosphere, and anyway Schoenberg wants the singer to use sprechgesang [1], a sort of half-speech/half-song effect which frankly makes the singer sound like an amateur who hasn't got her act together.

This is a highly misleading statement. *Pierrot Lunaire* is extremely chromatic, but was composed some years before the development of serialism.

In spite of the error regarding serialism, the observation about chromaticism is accepted here.

Examiner's points

There were six general observations here in a piece that was not entirely relevant. It would be awarded 6/13.

> **Exercise**
>
> Rewrite the first paragraph to provide the reader with more reliable historical context.

Sample answer 3

Mark this answer yourself, commenting at the end on its good points, but also mentioning ways in which it could have been improved. Check your assessment against the examiner's points which follow after completing your marking.

> Features contributing to disorientation and disturbance are:
> - Atonality. This produces an intentionally unstable sound. There is no fixed point in the music which allows the listener to feel secure.
> - This suits the subject matter which concerns the 'deathly sick moon of night' with pale blood born of torment.
> - To emphasise the unhinged nature of the text, Schoenberg uses Sprechgesang, a sort of speech-song which often involves notes being voiced in such a way that the pitch is uncertain, i.e. unstable.
> - The vocal writing is intentionally awkward with large leaps, made all the more difficult by the absence of a full harmonic accompaniment.

Examiner's points

The candidate made five clear points: atonality, subject matter, Sprechgesang, large leaps and lack of harmonic support. Unfortunately, the response stopped dead in its tracks after a promising start, and could only be awarded 6/13. It made a pleasant change to see Sprechgesang with an upper case S!

> **Exercise**
>
> Finish off the above response, providing also some supporting references for the point about large leaps. Try to make the last bullet point a summarising, concluding remark.

SAMPLE QUESTION 2

'Flying Theme' (NAM 45) is one of the most memorable sections of Williams' score for *ET*. What aspects of the melody and structure contribute to the music's staying power? (13)

Before studying the mark scheme (indicative content) which follows, attempt the question yourself. Notice that the key words are 'memorable', 'melody' and 'structure'. You may find it convenient to refer briefly to the dramatic context of the music, but take care to keep your remarks focused on melody and structure.

Indicative content	
Points should be illustrated with examples from the music.	
Melody	• Balanced eight-bar sections • Two-bar phrases • Often with same rhythm • Loosely sequential • Outlines common chords • Commanding large intervals and turn • Mainly diatonic.
Structure	• Repetitive scheme involving alternation of main and secondary theme • Variations in orchestration • And tonality, e.g. appearance of main theme in dominant.

Notice the use of transposing instruments in this score:	
Clarinet in B♭	Sounds a major 2nd below written pitch
Horn in F	Sounds a perfect 5th below written pitch
Trumpet in B♭	Sounds a major 2nd below written pitch

Sample answer 1

The structure of *ET* is simple repetition of a principal
theme [1], heard for the first time at bars 9–16,
immediately repeated at bar 17 [1]. It returns at bars
34–41 in G major, the dominant [1], then again at bars
56–62 in the tonic where it is further varied by imitation
in the horn [1], after which there is a coda.   ◄——— Accept: a good point.
    The fact that the theme is repeated so often makes it
easier to remember, and the theme itself is also
uncomplicated as it is periodically phrased in sets of two
bars [1], with rhythmic repetition, e.g. bars 11–12 have the
same rhythm as bars 9–10 [1]. The main melody has only
a little chromaticism [1], and the big tune has large leaps, ◄——— Accept for 'mainly diatonic' in the mark scheme.
typically perfect 5ths and octaves [1], resulting in a
powerful effect. The strong impression it creates is
further enhanced by use of the bright-sounding Lydian
scale, shown by the F♯ in bars 75 onwards [1].

Examiner's points

There are nine credit-worthy observations, most of them illustrated where possible.
The work is systematic and logical and would gain 13/13.

Exercise

Provide examples of any leap of a perfect 5th and larger.

Sample answer 2

- Children's sci-fi film about friendship of 10-year old boy and the extra-terrestrial
- Flying theme – written for a 'set-piece' scene with Elliot and ET going for a bike ride in the sky as the sun sets on Halloween ←

All true, but as yet nothing specific has been said about melody or structure.

- Minimalist intro, leading into
- Main theme in C ←

Not enough information yet for a mark.

- Repeated throughout the piece [1]
- Becomes Lydian near the end [1] ←

Point accepted.

- Structure repetitive ←

Point already made.

- Some changes in melody and key ←
- Tonal and approachable – different in mood from *On the Waterfront* ←

More information required.

- Quite dissonant harmony – see sus4 in bar 3 – so a bit more complicated than it first seems ←

Irrelevant.

- Huge orchestra helps strengthen sound – bells added ←

Irrelevant.

- Another dissonance is the false relation at bar 74

Not enough precise detail for credit.

- Tension built up by use of pedals
- Feeling of pedalling given by repetitive rhythms. ←

True, but irrelevant.

The final two points are irrelevant.

Examiner's points

The candidate made two relevant remarks, and would be awarded 2/13 ('inadequate').

Exercise

Write one sentence to establish the context of this music; then list a further six points which the candidate could have made.

Sample answer 3

Mark this answer yourself, commenting at the end on its good points, but also mentioning ways in which it could have been improved. Check your assessment against the examiner's points which follow after completing your marking.

The music of ET: *Flying Theme* is less to do with background effects than creating a single, sustained mood to accompany the famous bicycle in the sky sequence from Spielberg's sci-fi film. It relies on clear melody lines for its effect, and this melody in itself is memorable. This aspect of the melody is down to its balanced structure of two-bar phrases, and the striking shape of the main theme which outlines the common chord of C major. It also has prominent intervals of 5ths and 8ths which in turn help to give a grand, spacious feel.

The other point is that you hear the theme repeatedly, with some slight changes in minor details, and also of key, e.g. the switch to D major at bar 35. There are also changes in orchestration, for example, the big theme at the start appears in upper strings and woodwinds in octaves, while the next time it is doubled by trumpets and bells. Bells also appear at the end with glittering effect. This bright sound is also partly to do with Williams's harmonies. He uses some old-fashioned chords, and such effects as the dominant pedal, false relation and the Lydian mode (i.e. the F♯) also produces a bright, memorable effect.

Examiner's points

Marks are awarded here for two-bar phrases, common chord of C major, 5ths and 8ths, repetition of melody, variation of orchestration in repetition and Lydian mode. The candidate's description of the modulation at bar 35 was incorrect; not all the points were illustrated, and there was a tendency to drift away from the demands of the question. An appropriate mark for this attempt would be 6/13 ('adequate').

Exercise

Provide illustrations for the points made above. Draw up revision notes for other aspects of this score, e.g. harmony, rhythm and texture.

INSTRUMENTAL MUSIC 2016 (SECTION C)

SAMPLE QUESTION 1

Compare and contrast the use of textures in the pieces listed below. (36)

➢   Holborne – Pavane 'The image of melancholy' and Galliard 'Ecce quam bonum' (NAM 13)

➢   J. S. Bach – Partita No. 4 in D, BWV 828: Sarabande and Gigue (NAM 21)

➢   *Four* (NAM 50) as recorded by the Miles Davis Quintet

Before studying the mark scheme (indicative content) which follows, attempt the question yourself. Notice that the key word is 'texture'. You may find it convenient to refer briefly to the context of each work, but take care to keep your remarks relevant.

Indicative content	
Points should be illustrated with examples from the music.	
Holborne	• Five-part polyphony • Equivalent voices • Generally contrapuntal • Some imitation • Imitation by inversion • Homophony in central section of Galliard • Bass part less active • Pedals.
Bach	Sarabande contains a variety of textures: • Chordal • Monophonic • Two-part • With melody accompanied by slower-moving bass • Free-voiced at cadences • Gigue is imitative/fugal • In three parts.
Four	• Melody-dominated homophony • Head has melody played by saxophone and trumpet in octaves • Piano plays chords • Double bass has walking bass line.

Sample answer 1

A span of three and a half centuries separates the composition of these works, so it is not surprising to find considerable differences in approach to the use of textures. These differences are further magnified by the selection of forces for each work.

Holborne's work is a characteristic example of Renaissance polyphony. Written for five [1] equal parts [1], it is mainly contrapuntal [1]. It involves some imitation [1], but these imitative points are far from easy to hear as Holborne often conceals entries by avoidance of preceding rests [1] or else by using inversions, e.g. bar 1 of Galliard in first and fourth lines [1]. Most of the lines are as lively and melodic as the others, though for harmonic reasons, the bass line is slower moving [1], and even includes pedal-points, e.g. bars 34–39 of the Pavane [1]. The one significant departure from this basic texture comes with the second section of the Galliard which is more homophonic [1].

Texture in Bach's keyboard pieces are more varied. For most of the Sarabande, he uses a two-part texture [1]. Periodically there are chordal passages, as in bar 1 [1], which is immediately followed by a single-line passage [1]. The melody covers a wide range of the keyboard, and uses *Fortspinnung*, a device whereby the melody is spun out by repetition, sequence, and various forms of intervallic variation. All of this makes for a livelier texture than in the Holborne.

Even livelier is the gigue. This is fugal [1], with a number of imitations at the start of each section before moving into a freer style. In fact this is not really a fugue, because it divides into two clear sections, both repeated, to give the traditional binary scheme – a sign of the Baroque era. The other Baroque feature is the tonality, with a modulation to the dominant at the end of the first section, and to other related keys as the movement goes on.

The texture of *Four* is not so contrapuntal – in fact it is homophonic [1], although the sax imitates the trumpet throughout the head. There are offbeat chords on piano throughout the piece [1], and later a walking bass for double bass [1], although this one hurtles along at breakneck speed. The melody is in the trumpet, and there are some very interesting effects, e.g. slides, ghost notes etc.

These works are typical of their respective eras, but instead of counterpoint, the complexity of *Four* arises from the fast-moving melody line and dense, chromatic harmonies.

Notice that the candidate uses the term polyphony here simply to refer to the combination of a number of separate melody lines, and uses contrapuntal in connection with their independence.

Good point.

Unfortunately, although true, the point about melodic writing is irrelevant.

Irrelevant.

This observation is also irrelevant.

This is incorrect. Although they have the same melodic line, the two instruments double each other an octave apart.

These effects come under the heading of melodic decoration.

Examiner's points

The candidate made 16 often well-illustrated points. Unfortunately, there was considerable irrelevance, and the opening point regarding selection of performing forces was not developed in the course of the essay. This work would be regarded as 'confident', but the digressions would result in its receiving a mark of 24/36.

Exercise

List additional relevant points that could have been made.

Sample answer 2

Four is quite different from the other two pieces as it is homophonic throughout with melody in the trumpet [1]. It is doubled in the Head by the saxophone to make the basic theme stick out. It is preceded by a drum intro and has piano chords [1]. These are typical of the be-bop style, as they are highly dissonant, with many substitution chords. A prominent feature of the work is the improvisation which goes throughout the piece, although it does not affect the texture which is much the same throughout.

> This is not precise enough. The candidate should say that the trumpet is doubled at the octave by the saxophone.

> True, but irrelevant.

The other two pieces are much more contrapuntal **[1+1 for each work]**. Bach uses two-part counterpoint throughout, with melodic writing in the top part. The gigue uses imitation [1], which is only to be expected it being a fugue. The second section kicks off with an inversion of the main theme [X], like many other jigs, and Bach goes on to use other devices like stretto [X].

> This observation is misleading, as there are various textures in the Sarabande.

> A misleading remark as Bach does not write fugally throughout this movement.

Holborne's works are typically Renaissance dances with the Galliard a sort of triple time version of the Pavane [X]. It was very common for dances to be paired together, as in keyboard pieces by Byrd and Gibbons. These dances are also quite stylish [X], with much less dance elements than musical. In fact they are so complicated it would be very difficult to dance to. Quite apart from that, they sound dead gloomy, and in any case, when performed on viles, you can hardly hear what's going on. The beat is far from clear.

> The candidate here means 'stylised', a term which denotes that, in this case, the dance-like aspects of the music, though present, are much weakened.

With the Holborne, theres a lot of counterpoint, with all the players doing their own thing. The writing is not particularly idiomatic, as these pieces can be played on any instrument. Theres some imitation in these peices [1], e.g. b. 34 and 35, top and middle lines. One thing Holborne has in common with *Four* is the chordal writing in the Galliard, which all goes to show that nothing much changes down the years.

> An unfortunate confusion of words here!

> Point already credited.

> This is not precisely located.

Examiner's points

The candidate made six relevant observations, with limited illustration. There were numerous errors, and the quality of written communication was ungainly at times. This work would come into the 'basic' category, and be awarded 15/36.

Exercise

Improve the quality of written communication of this essay.

Sample answer 3

Mark this answer yourself, commenting at the end on its good points, but also mentioning ways in which it could have been improved. Check your assessment against the examiner's points which follow after completing your marking.

Textures change from one period to another and from one work to another, even within the same period. One of the factors which influences the use of textures is the instruments being used. The Holborne is for five instruments and therefore has a thick texture, while the Bach is for harpsichord and therefore sounds thin, and *Four* is for a much more varied group of performers (drums, sax, trumpet, piano and double bass) and so has plenty going on, but not quite as much as Holborne.

So starting with the Holborne, it is quite contrapuntal most of the time. There are five parts, all rather vocal in style, because the music dated from the period before instruments had developed their own techniques. As it says in the Anthology, these pieces can be performed on violins, viols or any musical wind instrument. (Note to examiner: I have translated this into proper English so you won't misunderstand.) In other words, these pieces can be played on any instruments, just so long the notes fit. Most of the parts play a similar role, but it is interesting to see that the bass part has less to do. Maybe he wasn't very good, or more likely it helped the harmony if there was a firm, clear support for what was going on above. The other parts tend to have a very similar style, and because the music is from the Renaissance period, it is contrapuntal. Sometimes he also uses imitations, and sometimes he uses inverted melody lines (see opening of Galliard).

Holborne departs from this approach only in bars 9–16 of the Galliard which is more chordal. This movement is in the minor key and closes with a tierce de Picardie as was customary at the time.

The Bach Sarabande includes a wide range of textures, starting with chords, before going on to a mainly two-part texture with the bass moving more slowly than the melody. In contrast, the gigue starts with a fugal passage with three parts coming in in imitation. Unlike the Holborne which is not idiomatic, this is now clearly intended for a keyboard player, and though it can be switched from harpsichord to piano — raising issues of authenticity — it obviously cannot be played on much else.

Finally, *Four*: this is now highly idiomatic with each instrument having a clearly defined role in the ensemble. The piano has chords supporting the incredibly fast-moving melody for trumpet, packed tight with technical devices which can only be played on that instrument. The bass provides a fast walking bass. The texture is best described as melody-dominated homophony.

Examiner's points

Credit is awarded for:

➢   Counterpoint in Holborne
➢   Five parts
➢   Slower moving bass part
➢   Imitation
➢   Inverted imitation
➢   Chords at the start of the Bach
➢   Two-part texture with slower moving bass
➢   Fugal opening of gigue
➢   Three parts
➢   Melody-dominated homophony in *Four*
➢   Walking bass
➢   Chords in piano.

The other points were irrelevant. Avoid asides to examiners, however helpful they are meant to be. This work was 'adequate', with 12 partially illustrated points, and would receive 19/36.

Exercise

Cut out the irrelevant remarks in Sample answer 3, and add six fully illustrated observations to help raise the score.

SAMPLE QUESTION 2

Compare and contrast the use of harmony and tonality in the three pieces listed below. (36)

➢   **Haydn – Symphony No. 26 in D minor, 'Lamentatione': movement I (NAM 2)**

➢   **Brahms – Piano Quintet in F minor, Op. 34: movement III (NAM 18)**

➢   **Duke Ellington and his Orchestra –** *Black and Tan Fantasy* **(NAM 49)**

Before studying the mark scheme (indicative content) which follows, attempt the question yourself. Notice that the key words are 'harmony' and 'tonality'. You may find it convenient to refer briefly to the context of each work, but take care to keep your remarks relevant.

Indicative content Points should be illustrated with examples from the music.		
Haydn	Harmony	• Functional progressions
		• Cadences (perfect and imperfect)
		• Circle of 5ths
		• Diminished 7th
		• Pedal points.
	Tonality	• Modulations to relative and tonic majors
		• Wider-ranging tonal scheme in development.
Brahms	Harmony	• Functional progressions
		• Secondary dominants
		• Pedal points
		• Chromatic chords, e.g. augmented 6ths
		• Occasional open-5th chords.
	Tonality	• Minor, with some modality
		• Wide-ranging key scheme.
Ellington	Harmony	• Based on 12-bar blues
		• Substitution chords
		• Circle of 5ths
		• Plagal cadence at close.
	Tonality	• Opens and closes in B♭ minor
		• Central passage in B♭ major.

Sample answer 1

Haydn was Classical, Brahms Romantic and Duke Ellington early 20th-century jazz. As about 170 years separates the earliest and latest works, it is only to be expected that there are certain differences between their approaches to harmony and tonality. Partly this is because of developments in forms and instrumentation. Haydn uses Sonata form for the first movement of the symphony, with a typical exposition of first and second subjects, a development where the themes are treated in various ways and then a recapitulation where everything comes back again. In contrast, Brahms uses a piano and solo strings instead of a classical orchestra, and the piece itself is a scherzo and trio, a massively expanded version of the minuet and trio, the sort of movement that Haydn would have written. In complete contrast, the Ellington piece is a 12-bar blues specially written to draw attention to problems of racial segregation.

> This over-extended introductory paragraph also introduces a number of irrelevant points. The first two sentences would have been sufficient to establish some sort of background.

When we come to a survey of harmony and tonality, the first thing to notice is the fact that Haydn uses functional harmony [1]. This means that the music is in major/minor keys rather than in modes or being atonal, and the chords help to define the keys through the use of cadences. There are four of these: imperfect, perfect, plagal and interrupted, though Haydn uses only the first two listed, e.g. the perfect cadence, consisting of a dominant to tonic progression, as at bar 16 [1]. The imperfect cadence also consists of two chords. The second is the dominant, but we cannot be sure of the first chord until we hear it, as any workable chord is acceptable here. Haydn uses an imperfect cadence at bars 98–99 [1]. Otherwise his choice of chords is quite limited.

> At last!

> At this level, it will be assumed that you know what the chord progressions making up the cadences are, and there really is no need to specify them.

> What is the term for this device?

Brahms uses a much wider selection, but there are times when there is hardly any harmony at all. This happens at the start where there is just a simple bass note accompanying the melody lines – a repeated C. When the chords come in at bar 22, Brahms changes to C major from F minor [X]. He also uses rhythmic augmentation here to produce a grand effect. The harmony here is rich, as all the instruments are playing. In fact there's a fantastic amount of harmony in the piano part as the pianist has to play lots of notes.

> A frequent misreading of the key at the opening of this movement. The quintet overall is in F minor, but this movement of course opens in C minor.

> Irrelevant.

> A nonsensical statement!

There are more passages without much harmony, like the fugato, which has just the viola to start with. At other places, it is difficult to work out the chords as Brahms

> This comment has more to do with texture.

uses quite advanced keys and lots of accidentals. It is the same with Duke Ellington. This piece is a 12-bar blues [1] which means you have chord I for four bars, chord IV for two bars, chord I for two bars, chord V for two bars and then chord I for two bars. After this, it just keeps repeating, except that here Ellington introduces a 16-bar section. He also uses substitution chords [1] to vary the basic progression. Another way of getting variety is at bar 13 where the music changes to Bb major [1]. Another variation comes at the end where there is a quote from Chopin's *Funeral March*.

As with the previous remarks on cadences, it is not necessary to spell out in detail the harmonic structure of 12-bar blues. You would only need to comment on irregularities.

This remark tells us nothing about the harmony or tonality.

Approaches to tonality vary considerably, and this is where the instrumentation comes in. Haydn wrote for a small Classical orchestra, with harpsichord, giving a light thin sound, but not much variety in tone quality. Brahms wrote for piano and solo strings, so although there are not so many players, the fact that they were more skilled and could cover a wider range, results in greater variation in tonality. Tonality is most varied in *Black & Tan Fantasy*, as Ellington has a much wider range of instruments, and so with the rhythm and reeds sections he could get much more contrast in tone colour.

The candidate has confused tonality – keys and modulation – with timbre, i.e. tone quality.

All this shows how harmony and tonality have changed down the years.

Examiner's points

The candidate made five points. There was extensive irrelevance and confusion, so under these circumstances the final mark would be in the region of 12/36.

Exercise

Write a paragraph contrasting the approaches to tonality in the three works under discussion.

Sample answer 2

Haydn's Symphony No 26 in D minor provides a good example of the workings of functional harmony and tonality [1]. Starting in D minor, the first subject of 16 bars is sealed off with a perfect cadence [1]. Immediately the music shifts to F major, the relative major [1], for the second subject. The development modulates through a wide range of keys [1], notably G minor at bar 55 [1] and A minor in the passage closing at bar 74 [1]. Other characteristic devices are the circle of fifths at bars 56–65 [1] and the dominant pedal starting at bar 65 [1]. One of the most dramatic harmonic effects comes at bar 69 with the diminished 7th [1]. The recapitulation at bar 80 is in D minor [1], and the second subject is heard this time in D major [1].

> No mark awarded for this, as the key is stated in the title.

Brahms's Quintet, written about 100 years later, is considerably more complex in both harmony and tonality. Starting in C minor [1], with a tonic pedal [1], the tonality is notable early on for its modal inflections, e.g. at bar 19 where Brahms avoids using the raised leading note [1]. At bar 22, there is a sudden shift to C major [1], and secondary dominants lead to brief references to A minor and G major [1]. Brahms then turns back towards C minor by way of an augmented-6th chord in bar 39 [1], but as the movement proceeds he touches on a much wider range of keys, e.g. G minor at bar 57 [1], E♭ minor at bar 67 [1], E♭ major at bar 110 [1]. The trio also touches on some unexpected keys. It opens in C major [1], but soon modulates to B major at bar 207 [1]. The return of the main theme at bar 242 is in a sort of destabilised C, with B♭ in the bass pulling it towards the subdominant [1]. A further striking tonal device comes at the close of the movement. As expected it closes on C, but because of the approach to the chord, this feels relatively weak, in fact more of a dominant preparation for the next movement in F [1].

> Good, perceptive comment.

In contrast, *Black and Tan Fantasy*, though perhaps no less complex harmonically than the Brahms, is certainly less enterprising in terms of tonality. It starts in B♭ minor [1], the largest part in the middle starting at bar 13 is in the tonic major [1], and the music returns to B♭ minor for the final four bars [1].

> Effective linking contrast.

The harmony is initially dictated by the 12-bar blues pattern [1], but as the piece unfolds, Ellington uses some unusual additional harmonies, e.g. the G♭7 at bar 13 which working as a German 6th leads onto the tonic B♭ major at bar 15 [1]. Other noteworthy features include the diminished 7th in bar 58 [1], the circle of 5ths at bars 19–21 [1] and the final string of plagal cadences [1].

> The mark is not for reading off the chord indication, but describing its function.

Examiner's points

The candidate made over 30 well illustrated points succinctly. (Compare this sample answer with the first.) The essay would have benefited from an introduction and conclusion, and so an appropriate mark would be 35/36.

Exercise

Provide a brief introduction and conclusion.

Sample answer 3

Mark this answer yourself, commenting at the end on its good points, but also mentioning ways in which it could have been improved. Check your assessment against the examiner's points which follow after completing your marking.

- Haydn's Symphony is in D minor. Brahms Piano Quintet is also in a minor key (C). Ellington's piece is also in a minor key (B♭ minor). All three pieces also have passages in major keys.
- Ellington uses substitution chords. The harmonies at the start are easy to see: B♭ minor, E♭ minor, B♭ minor, F, B♭ minor, E♭ minor, B♭ minor, G♭, B♭, E♭7, B♭, C7, F7, then nothing happens for the rest of the page.
- Haydn doesn't use substitution chords, but he does use diminished 7ths. Brahms modulates to C major at bar 22. Ellington finishes with a plagal cadence. Haydn doesn't use plagal cadences, but he finishes with a perfect cadence.
- Brahms uses remote keys like B major.
- Ellington uses substitute chords. Unlike Ellington, Haydn finishes in D major. Brahms opens with a tonic pedal – the repeated Cs in the cello. Ellington's piece is a sort of variation piece built on the 12-bar blues.

- Haydn uses a circle of 5ths at bar 56. So does Ellington. Brahms doesn't.
- Ellington uses pitch bends to vary the harmonies. Haydn also uses a dominant pedal.

Examiner's points

Marks can be awarded here for:

➢ Naming the keys of the Piano Quintet and *Black and Tan Fantasy*

➢ Use of substitution chords in *Black and Tan Fantasy*

➢ Diminished 7ths in Haydn

➢ Modulation to C at bar 22 in the Piano Quintet

➢ Plagal cadence at the close of *Black and Tan Fantasy*

➢ Perfect cadence at the end of Haydn's movement

➢ D major at the close of the Haydn

➢ Tonic pedal in the Brahms

➢ 12-bar blues in the Ellington

➢ Circle of 5ths in the Haydn.

Notice that credit was not awarded for key references which were not located precisely, reading off the chord descriptions from the score of *Black and Tan Fantasy*, and negative statements.

There was no evidence of planning, the whole piece being little more than a random stringing together of facts, not all of which were fully illustrated.

As there were 11 points with limited illustration, but weak organisation, this piece would be awarded 16/36.

Exercise

Organise Sample answer 3, grouping points together logically and providing bar references where appropriate.

Exercise

Using your study guides and any other sources you have, draw up revision notes for all the instrumental works for 2016, making sure you are equipped to write on rhythm, metre, melody, harmony, tonality, structure, texture and general context and circumstances of performance.

APPLIED MUSIC 2017 (SECTION B)

SAMPLE QUESTION 1

Describe those aspects of *Morse on the Case* that make it suitable as a piece of incidental music for a television drama. (13)

Before studying the mark scheme (indicative content) that follows, attempt the question yourself.

Indicative content	
Function	The music is designed to be both atmospheric and unobtrusive.
Dynamics	Generally soft throughout.
Resources	Limited to strings, harp, piano, oboe and four horns.
Rhythm	Little movement; lengthy, sustained notes; little sense of pulse; silent bar.
Melody	• Limited amount of melodic material • Mainly diatonic, with few chromatic notes • Gradual unfolding of lines built of perfect 4ths, minor 3rds, major 2nds • Although difficult to hear, there is use of e.g. inversion and diminution (reflecting the thoughtful side of the main character).
Harmony and tonality	• There is no sense of functional progression or a strong drive to cadence • 'Harmony' consists mainly of verticalisations of the component intervals (i.e. chords composed of the notes of the basic motifs) • It is therefore mildly dissonant for the most part • The chromatic notes, especially A♭, produce more stringent clashes, with e.g. A♭ in oboe and A♮ in viola at bars 93–95 (perhaps indicating an intensification in the dramatic situation) • The excerpt eventually moves from A Aeolian to a C major chord at bar 110 (perhaps hinting at a possible resolution in the drama) • But the F♯s, e.g. bars 105 and 108, perhaps suggest the Lydian mode (indicating a brightening of the prevailing mood) • The final chord is ambiguous as it lacks the 3rd.
Structure	There is no discernible structure; the excerpt appears to be through-composed to reflect the on-screen events.
Texture	Pheloung avoids tutti passages, with a sparing use of resources being evident throughout: • Upper strings play throughout, but cellos and bass appear only at bar 99 • Piano plays intermittently throughout, playing variously single notes, two notes, parallel 9ths (bar 36), and five notes on one occasion (bar 98) • The four horns are only used together from bar 98.

Sample answer 1

The music is unobtrusive so it does not overwhelm the screen action [1]. This subtle approach is evident in:
1. The limited number of instruments [1]
2. The generally soft dynamics [1]
3. The lack of a strong, distracting pulse [1]
4. The very limited amount of melodic material [1]
5. The vague harmonisations and tonal scheme [X – not enough], and the chord without a 3rd at the end [1 – illustrated point].

Examiner's points

The candidate sets up the makings of a sound answer with the opening assertion and series of follow-up points. Unfortunately, there is an absence of substantiating information and examples, and so the mark is not as high as it could have been. The candidate made six points with limited illustration, and so the final mark would be **6/13**.

Exercise
Suggest some ways in which the main points could have been elaborated.

Sample answer 2

Mark this answer yourself, commenting at the end on its good points, but also mentioning ways in which it could have been improved. After completing your marking, check your assessment against the examiner's points below.

Pheloung provided music for all the Morse dramas, and established a distinctive and effective approach to the writing of incidental music for detective programmes. Pheloung's music is almost self-effacing. Apart from the well-known signature tune, based on Morse code, there is nothing which attracts immediate attention. The music fades in and out as required, and the dynamic level is always soft. The rhythmic scheme is hardly discernible. Notes are long, often being tied across several bars, and it is virtually impossible to detect first beats of the bar or any other strong stresses.

It is also difficult to detect melodic shapes. It is only when you look at the score that you can appreciate the way Pheloung developed the limited number of motifs he employs. At the start there is a simultaneous inversion of the opening motif made up of intervals of a rising 4th and falling minor 3rd, while later he diminishes the cell made up of 2nds and 4ths (see bar 26).

Just as the rhythms and motifs are rather indeterminate, the approach to harmony and tonality is vague. There is in fact little clear harmony, the lines simply coming together at times. Dissonances are far from harsh, with only the Ab on oboe really clashing as it is a chromatic note within the prevailing Aeolian mode. At the end there is perhaps more clarity as the music shifts from A to C, but it is difficult to detect much of a tonal centre. The F♯ perhaps makes it seem like the Lydian mode for a moment, but the final chord which lacks a 3rd makes it impossible to detect a prevailing mode.

Because of the unobtrusive nature of the writing, Pheloung's score is ideal as incidental music, especially for stories that focus on the musings of the central character.

Examiner's points

This was a good, sound attempt, and credit could be awarded for the following points:

➢ 'Self-effacing… nothing which attracts immediate attention'

➢ Soft dynamic level throughout (location given)

➢ Hardly discernible rhythms with long notes and their effects on the stress scheme (not located)

➢ Difficulty in detecting melodic shapes and the limited number of motifs

➢ Simultaneous inversion at the start (location given)

➢ Diminution (illustrated point)

➢ Random harmonic movement

➢ Chromatic Ab (not located)

➢ Aeolian mode

➢ C Lydian at the end (location given)

➢ Final chord without a 3rd (location given).

The essay would be awarded a mark of **11–12/13**. The writing was good, and there was evidence of careful planning and organisation.

Exercise

The candidate did not mention structure or use of resources. Insert a further paragraph to cover these aspects of the music.

SAMPLE QUESTION 2

Diaghilev asked Stravinsky for arrangements of various 18th-century works for the ballet score of *Pulcinella*. Focusing on harmony and texture in 'Gavotta con due variazioni' *(NAM 7)*, offer reasons for Diaghilev's initial shocked reaction to the result. (13)

Before studying the mark scheme (indicative content) that follows, attempt the question yourself. Notice that the key words are 'harmony', 'texture', 'Gavotta con due variazioni' and 'shocked reaction'. You may find it convenient to refer briefly to the historical context, but take care to keep your remarks relevant. Do not waste time on any aspect of the Gavotta that is not related to harmony and texture.

Indicative content	
Harmony	• Functional framework (derived from the original works) with perfect cadences. Original works are modified by addition of pedals and horn appoggiaturas. Other noteworthy features: • Bar 43: tonic chord clashes with subdominant chord • Bar 51: unprepared dissonance in oboe 2 line • Bar 69: modulation to A major weakened by ambiguous G♮ in bassoon 1 • Bar 76: unprepared dissonance in flute • Bar 79: oboe 1 has new countermelody creating suspensions • Bars 80 and 83: weakened perfect cadences, with partial resolution and changes of register.
Texture	• Scored for wind and brass instruments only. Instrumentation aimed at producing typical neoclassical, non-expressive, anti-Romantic sound. • The original basic two-part texture is expanded by addition of countermelodies (e.g. horn in bar 39, oboe 2 at bar 50). Other features: • Additional accompaniment figuration; sustained notes; glissandi in bassoon; Alberti bass in bassoon; rapid runs in the two flutes.

Examiners arrive at a final mark for these questions using a holistic grid. For full details see Edexcel's *Sample Assessment Materials*. For the present, it is enough to know that the full 13 marks will be awarded to work that contains at least nine relevant, well-illustrated points, showing excellent organisation and planning, and expressed coherently without significant spelling or grammatical errors.

As you work through this section of the book, and see examples of work of different standards, you will see how the holistic grid is applied across the available mark range.

Sample answer 1

Harmony in the *Gavotta* is basically traditional, as is the form which is binary. The first section, up to the repeat sign at bar 10, starts in D and as expected moves to A major, and the second section modulates more widely. There is a section in G to begin with, then a sequential repeat in A, then a series of cadences in F# minor, E minor and D. The variations all follow the same pattern. ◄

Cadences also follow traditional 'functional' patterns [1] with e.g. imperfect cadences in bars 4 and 10 [X]. ◄

There are also many examples of 'wrong-note' harmony which was typical of the neoclassical style developed in the 1920s [1]. There is a glaring clash at the beginning of the *Gavotta*, where the horn C# is heard against the D in the oboe [X – **the candidate has forgotten that the horn is a transposing instrument**].

Textures are also quite different from the original by Monza, which was mainly in two parts. Stravinsky scored this movement for woodwinds and brass, seeking to avoid the over-emotional sonorities of the string section [1]. Because he included many more instruments, the textures are obviously thicker, and ◄ they become even more thick when Stravinsky adds extra lines, especially obvious in Variation 1 at bar 50 where the second oboe is given a new part [1 – **illustrated point**].

In many ways, Stravinsky retains original aspects of the Monza with trills and the like, though he does sometimes make the melody jerkier than it was in the 18th-century version.

> There is much good detail here, but alas it is all irrelevant. 'Traditional' harmony is not precise enough at this level to gain credit, and strictly speaking modulation and changes of key come under the heading of tonality.

> One of the striking aspects about the harmony of the Gavotta is that all the cadences are perfect.

> Try to avoid 'thick' and 'thin' as descriptions of textures at this level.

Examiner's points

The candidate made four partly illustrated points. The answer was well-written, but marred by irrelevance. Harmony should primarily concern chord structure, chord progressions (including cadences) and dissonance treatment. The answer would gain a mark of **5/13**.

Exercise

Help the candidate raise their mark by suggesting a further two harmonic and two textural points, with appropriate illustrations.

Sample answer 2

Mark this answer yourself, commenting at the end on its good points, but also mentioning ways in which it could have been improved. After completing your marking, check your assessment against the examiner's points below.

Stravinsky's score is the first of his neoclassical works, and the start of what proved to be the longest creative phase of his career, lasting over 30 years and culminating with *The Rake's Progress* in 1951.

There were already hints of this style in the preceding years, e.g. *The Soldier's Tale*, so it could be said that Diaghilev should have realised what he was in for.

The basis for *Pulcinella* was a series of pieces by Gallo, Pergolesi and Monza, among others, but instead of simply arranging them, Stravinsky 're-composed' them, as he put it.

Gavotta and two variations was based on a keyboard work by Monza, and its basic two-part texture was expanded for the woodwind and brass sections of the band. Stravinsky had already used this sort of group in his *Symphonies for Wind Instruments*, and many other works of the 1920s make more use of these parts of the orchestra at the expense of the strings, e.g. the *Piano Concerto* and *Symphony of Psalms*, as part of an anti-Romantic reaction.

The expansion of the original to involve several instruments meant additional melody lines and doublings. Some of these additions include the Alberti bass in Variation 2, the rapid runs in the flute and the additional melody lines, e.g. the horn figures in the main theme at bar 11 and the additional oboe lines at bar 51.

Stravinsky also introduced some unusual timbres, notably the glissando effects in the bassoon and the rather high horn parts.

Many of the textural additions have some bearing on the harmony. Inevitably, this is basically traditional with cadential progressions, all of which are perfect. But the cadences are frequently undermined, e.g. right at the end which fizzles out with an open octave, while in the first-time bar, the dominant chord is not followed by a full tonic chord, but a thinly textured return to the Alberti figuration.

Other ways that Stravinsky peps up the harmony involve the adding of pedals, e.g. at bars 26–28, where the inverted tonic pedal sounds right through the perfect cadence, including the dominant chord. Elsewhere he allows a complete clash of D and G chords (bar 44). Additional lines, such as the oboe in bar 51, introduce random unprepared dissonances which sound mildly shocking.

Diaghilev may have been shocked by what Stravinsky did to the 18th-century material, but the result is a great introduction to a particular type of 20th-century style, perfectly matching the mischievous onstage action.

Examiner's points

This well-written account provided good historical context, and incidentally linked the additional textural elements to the harmonic style. The credit-worthy points were:

➤ Woodwind and brass instrumentation

➤ Anti-Romantic reaction

➤ Alberti bass (location given)

➤ Rapid flute runs (not located)

➤ Additional melody lines (illustrated point)

➤ Bassoon glissandi (not located)

➤ High horn parts (not located)

➤ Perfect cadences (not located)

➤ Undermining of cadences (illustrated point)

➤ Pedals (illustrated point)

➤ Superimposed D and G chords (location given)

➤ Unprepared dissonance (location given).

There were 12 points, some of which were illustrated. The essay would gain full marks.

Exercise

Collect information on the harmony and texture in the Sinfonia and Vivo.

INSTRUMENTAL MUSIC 2017 (SECTION C)

SAMPLE QUESTION 1

Compare and contrast the use of melody and texture in the works listed below (36).

➤ **Sweelinck – *Pavana Lachrimae***

➤ **Corelli – Trio Sonata in D, Op. 3 No. 2: movement IV**

➤ **Shostakovich – String Quartet No. 8, Op. 110: movement I**

Before studying the mark scheme (indicative content) that follows, attempt the question yourself. Notice that the key words are 'melody' and 'texture'. You may find it convenient to refer briefly to the context of each work, but take care to keep your remarks relevant. Points should be illustrated with examples (i.e. bar references) from the music.

Indicative content	
Melody	**Sweelinck** • Transfer of vocal styles to keyboard • Extensive conjunct movement • Descending ('falling tears') line spanning a perfect 4th, sometimes a diminished 4th • Rapid semiquaver ornamentation of melodic material • Notated trills • Minor key with modal elements and variable scales • Occasional use of sequence. **Corelli** Major key; mainly 3rds and stepwise movement; fragmentation; inversion; sequence. **Shostakovich** In a low tessitura throughout; often chromatic; DSCH motif; quotations from earlier works (e.g. Symphony No. 1); appoggiaturas; conjunct movement; narrow-range motives; repetition; sequence.
Texture	**Sweelinck** Idiomatic keyboard style, involving a range of textures: free counterpoint; imitation of melody in inner parts; antiphony/dialogue between 6ths in right hand and 3rds in left hand; three-part imitation. **Corelli** Polarised; fugal elements; some homorhythm; stretto. **Shostakovich** • Low tessituras throughout • Four-part imitation • DSCH in octaves with internal pedal on viola • Two-part counterpoint • Homophony • Drone and melody in violin I • Pedal supporting accompanying figures and melody • Chord in upper parts with melody in cello • Four-part free counterpoint.

Sample answer 1

The basic melody in Sweelinck's *Pavana Lachrimae* is actually by Dowland, being originally a pavane to which he fitted the words of *Flow My Tears*. Appropriately, it is in minor mode with modal inflections [1], and is typified by falling stepwise lines [1], representing the falling lines of the verse. There are occasional expressive leaps, e.g. the rising minor 6th in bar 2 [1 – **illustrated point**]. Sweelinck's contribution was to provide a variation for each strain involving rapid semiquaver runs [1].

In contrast Corelli's melodic lines are in a major key [1], and generally consist of a combination of stepwise movement and relatively small leaps – most usually 3rds [1]. Corelli extends the line with sequences [1] and also uses inversion in bar 20 [1 – **location given**].

In his String Quartet, Shostakovich uses a cipher based on his own initials [1] – D is short for Dmitry, and he arrives at E♭ as in German musical notation it is called Es, which gives him the S. C is C and B♮ is H. This gives SCH at the end of the German form of his name. Another famous cipher is B♭–A–C–B♮ which spells Bach. Shostakovich also draws on some of his other works, for example, Symphony No. 1 at bar 19 [1 – **illustrated point**] and a descending line taken from Symphony No. 5 [1 – **illustrated point**]. The reason for this self-quotation was perhaps because the quartet almost became a suicide note as Shostakovich was depressed at having been forced to join the Russian communist party. Given the gloomy nature of the background to the work, ◄— it is not surprising that the melodies are often in a minor key [1] and use expressive features such as appoggiaturas [1].

The extensive commentary on ciphers and the autobiographical origins of the work are out of proportion in an essay of this scope. Always try to keep remarks relevant.

Textures in Sweelinck's work vary throughout. The *Pavana* opens with a sort of melody and accompaniment with the accompaniment in a form of free counterpoint [1]. In the middle section there is dialogue between the hands [1] and imitation [1]. ◄—

Apart from giving bar references, there is more to be said about the dialogue, e.g. the intervals used in the right hand as opposed to the left. In the case of the imitation, how many voices are involved?

Corelli's Trio Sonata has a typical Baroque polarised texture, with two high violin parts and a much lower bass part [1]. As is usual, the bass is doubled by a continuo instrument, in this case an organ, which supplies supporting harmonies [1]. Again, there is a variety of textures, ranging from imitation [1], homorhythm [1] and stretto [1].

Shostakovich's quartet is also highly varied. It opens imitatively with a series of entries built on DSCH [1 – **location given**]. There are passages involving two-part counterpoint [1], and also a lengthy section of melody with drone [1]. The very low instrumental ranges also contribute to the gloom which is typical of this movement [1].

Examiner's points

Apart from a couple of excessively longwinded digressions, much of this essay was clearly focused on the demands of the question. The candidate made 25 relevant observations, but unfortunately not all of these were adequately substantiated. In view of this, the essay would be considered 'confident', and be awarded a mark in the region of **25/36**.

Exercise

Provide an introduction and conclusion to the essay.

Sample answer 2

Mark this answer yourself, commenting at the end on its good points, but also mentioning ways in which it could have been improved. After completing your marking, check your assessment against the examiner's points below.

Though nearly four centuries separate the composition of the earliest and latest works in this question, there are remarkable similarities in approaches to both melody and texture.

Sweelinck was well-acquainted with the work of a number of English composers who worked on the continent, and there is good reason to believe he adopted some of the keyboard techniques of such composers as John Bull in his own writing. Not only that, he used as the basis for *Pavana Lachrimae* the lute-song 'Flow my tears' by the English composer John Dowland, who also spent some time abroad, mainly at the Danish court.

The melancholy atmosphere of *Pavana Lachrimae*, like that of the original it was based on, lies partly in the use of the minor key and the measured pace associated with the pavane. The melodic lines fall by step, so symbolising the falling tears of Dowland's text. In addition there are sequential repeats, for example bars 2–4 are a higher version of the line in bars 1–2. There is also in bar 2 an expressive leap of a minor 6th.

In effect, Sweelinck was limited by Dowland's material, but he repeated each strain with variations that feature running semiquavers and ornamentations, such as the written-out trill in bar 14.

The textures in *Pavana Lachrimae* go beyond a simple melody-and-accompaniment. At the start the lower parts are freely contrapuntal, and later on there is antiphonal exchange between the hands at bar 40, where the 6ths in the right hand answer the 3rds in the left. There is also imitation for three of the four parts at bar 43 onwards.

Melody in Sweelinck's piece is obviously vocal in origin, whereas in Corelli it is much more idiomatic. It covers a wide range, though at any one time it tends to involve conjunct movement or intervals of a 3rd. Corelli breaks up the main theme, for example the quaver motif picked out at bar 11, and also uses inversion (bar 20) and sequence (bars 8–10). The textures seem at first to be fugal, as violin II comes in with a sort of answer, and there is also use of stretto at bar 21 where the subject comes in after only one bar.

The melody in the Shostakovich is sometimes based on the DSCH cipher – D, Eb, C, B – which stands for an abbreviation of the composer's name. It appears at the start in a series of imitative entries, starting with the lowest of the four instruments. It also appears in a purely homophonic texture (bar 79). Shostakovich also uses a melody and drone. His melodies are often chromatic, and so differ greatly from Corelli's.

Examiner's points

The candidate here provided a large amount of relevant information, with credit being earned for:

Sweelinck:

➤ Falling conjunct lines
➤ Ornamentation (illustrated)
➤ Sequence (illustrated)
➤ Freely contrapuntal at the start (located)
➤ Minor 6th (located)
➤ Antiphony at bar 40 (located)
➤ Running semiquavers
➤ Imitation at bar 43 (located).

Corelli:

➤ Conjunct writing, with 3rds
➤ Sequence (located)
➤ Breaking up of main theme (illustrated)
➤ Fugal textures
➤ Inversion (located)
➤ Stretto (located).

Shostakovich:

➤ DSCH
➤ Melody and drone
➤ Imitative entries (located)
➤ Chromaticism.
➤ Homophony (located)

Many of these points were substantiated by way of bar references. Unfortunately, the candidate perhaps spent so much time establishing the background to Sweelinck's approach that they seemed to run out of time. A number of additional points could have been made in the final paragraphs, and the essay would have benefited from some concluding remarks. It would however fall into the 'excellent' category, and earn a mark in the region of **27/36**.

Exercise

Shorten the second paragraph, provide some further information on Shostakovich and write a concluding paragraph.

SAMPLE QUESTION 2

Compare and contrast the use of rhythm and harmony in the works listed below. (36)

➢   **Berlioz – *Harold in Italy*: movement III**

➢   **Cage – *Sonatas and Interludes for Prepared Piano*: Sonatas I–III**

➢   **Ram Narayan (India) – *Rag Bhairav***

Before studying the mark scheme (indicative content) that follows, attempt the question yourself. Notice that the key words are 'rhythm' and 'harmony'. You may find it convenient to refer briefly to the context of each work, but take care to keep your remarks relevant. Points should be illustrated with examples (i.e. bar references) from the music. At a basic level you could just list relevant features of each work, but you may like to try to go further by drawing attention to common features (e.g. stating whether all of the works use drones).

Indicative content	
Rhythm	**Berlioz** • Opens with $\frac{6}{8}$ saltarello dance rhythms, with frequent dotted rhythms and stresses on the second beat of the bar • The second section is in a slower $\frac{6}{8}$ with some bars appearing to be in $\frac{3}{4}$ • The idée fixe is in longer notes, chiefly dotted minims • All rhythmic elements are heard together at bar 166 • Augmentation in bars 192–193.

	Cage
	• Inaudible fractal/micro-macrocosmic scheme in which small-scale rhythmic durations determine the overall proportions of the structure
	• Sonata I uses seven-crotchet units in sets of 4 1 3 (repeated); 4 2 (repeated)
	• Sonata II: 1½ + 1½ + 2⅜ + 2⅜ applied to 31 crotchets
	• Sonata III: 1 + 1 + 3¼ + 3¼ applied to 34 crotchets
	• At surface level, the sonatas are marked by: off-beat effects; triplets; other irregular note groupings; rhythmic displacements of short patterns; frequent changes of time signature.
	Rag Bhairav
	• The piece moves from slow, rhythmically free improvisation to music with a clear pulse and energetic rhythmic patterns:
	• Lines 1–13: rhythmically free section (alap)
	• Lines 14–18: jhor with more discernible pulse
	• Lines 19–end: jhala with tabla.
	• The tal here is based on a tintal (16-beat rhythmic cycle), subdivided into four vibhag of four beats each
	• Increasingly florid elaborations involve: various types of dotted rhythm; triplets; shorter note values; 'irregular' groupings.
Harmony	**Berlioz**
	Functional, with cadences; double pedal (drone) in saltarello; secondary 7ths; diminished 7ths; chromaticism.
	Cage
	Traditional harmonic procedures are impossible because of the effects of preparation. There are no cadences, and only occasional discernible chord structures:
	• The opening 7th chord of Sonata I
	• The parallel chords in Sonata I (bar 20).
	Rag Bhairav
	There is properly speaking no harmony as such, only the drone provided by the tampura.

Sample answer 1

This selection of works makes for an interesting set of comparisons, though whether anything useful will emerge is a completely different matter. Naturally the methods of these composers are bound to be radically opposed to each other as they come from different periods and backgrounds: Berlioz as a 19th-century Romantic, Cage as one of the most anti-traditional composers of the 20th century, and the Rag as an example of Northern Indian chamber music.

> A fair opening paragraph, quickly establishing some context.

Rhythm in the Berlioz is initially governed by the choice of the saltarello dance as the basis of the outer sections of the movement [1]. In $\frac{6}{8}$, it is typified by lively dotted rhythms [1] and occasional off-beat stresses [1]. The central portion of the movement – the serenade proper – moves at a more sedate pace and involves running semiquavers in some of the accompaniment part as well as the solo viola line [1]. The viola also introduces the idée fixe in much longer notes [1]. One of the most striking parts of the movement comes when Berlioz superimposes the saltarello melody and rhythms with the serenade and the idée fixe [1].

> These are valid points, but remember to give bar numbers wherever possible for substantiating examples!

In the Berlioz symphony, rhythm is only one of many elements, but in Cage's Sonatas it is almost the dominant feature. Time signatures are constantly changing [1], and Cage also applies a fractal system, a micro-macrocosmic approach which means that rhythmic proportions also control the structure [1]. In the case of Sonata I, this is seven crotchet units in sets of 4:1:3 (repeated) and 4:2 (repeated) which leads to an opening section of 28 beats (bars 1–7), followed by one bar of only seven crotchets, and then bars 9–12 amounting to 21 beats [1 – **illustrated point**].

> A good connecting idea.

Rhythm is put to different use in *Rag Bhairav*. The first part (lines 1–13) is a rhythmically free improvisation where the main melodic ideas are announced [1]. As the piece progresses, the rhythmic drive intensifies, first in the Jhor [1], and finally in the Jhala, where the tabla is introduced [1 – **location given**]. The tabla provides a tal, or rhythmic cycle of 16 beats, consisting of four sets of four [1]. Rhythms here become increasingly lively, with sometimes irregular groupings [1].

> The location here – 'in the Jhor' – is not sufficiently precise.

> Reference to the entry of the tabla indirectly gives the location.

Harmony in the Berlioz is initially affected by the use of the saltarello in order to show the folk origins of the dance. This is clear from the drone on C and G which runs through the first 31 bars [1 – **illustrated point**], over which Berlioz uses a limited range of chords. In the Serenade, more conventional harmonies occur, but Berlioz does not always follow the expected progressions [1]. ◄——— Examples would be good here.

In the final stages, effective use is made of a much more relaxed harmonic rhythm, and in fact the harmonic element seems to be faded out of the music before the end [1 – **accept**].

In the case of Cage, it is much more difficult to discuss harmony. The preparations to the piano often so distort the sounds that the written chords sound completely different from what was expected [1]. Harmony is most evident in Sonata I. It opens with what look like 7th chords on G [1 – **illustrated point**], and at the end there is a stream of parallel chords [1 – **illustrated point**], which here do sound more or less as might be expected. Elsewhere, there is scarcely anything truly harmonic.

In *Rag Bhairav*, the only harmonic device is the drone which supports the melodic material throughout [1 – **location given**].

Examiner's points

This was a sound attempt, standing on the borderline between 'confident' and 'excellent'. 21 points were made, but not all of them were fully illustrated. In terms of organisation, it would have been a good idea to try to draw the threads together in a concluding paragraph, so ensuring a higher mark within the relevant band. In other respects, it was well-constructed. It would receive a mark in the region of **27/36**.

Exercise

Provide a concluding paragraph. You could try to draw threads together by commenting on the Indian influence on Cage, and the extent to which they are reflected in the Sonatas. Are there any common features linking *Harold in Italy* with *Rag Bhairav*?

Sample answer 2

Mark this answer yourself, commenting at the end on its good points, but also mentioning ways in which it could have been improved. After completing your marking, check your assessment against the examiner's points below.

It is surprising to observe the number of links between these widely differing works. *Rag Bhairav* and *Harold in Italy*: movement III immediately seem to have one thing in common: a drone that accompanies their melodic material. In the case of *Rag Bhairav*, it is present throughout, and so there is effectively no harmonic progression as such, so leaving the music to develop entirely through melodic and rhythmic elements. In the case of the Cage, there also seems to be something like a drone at the start of Sonata III, but because of the preparation of the piano you can never be sure of what you are hearing. It does not go on for very long either, and generally there is not much in the way of proper harmony in Cage's pieces. There is two-part writing in Sonata II and three strands towards the end, but it is only in Sonata I that he writes proper chords, such as the G^7 at the start and the series of parallel chords.

The rhythmic element is important in all three works, but is used in very different ways. It is probably most exciting in *Rag Bhairav*, as the players move from free ad-libbing in the first section to increasingly wild and fast rhythms at the end, evident as the tabla comes in. The tabla part is nothing like as complicated as some others, consisting of recurring 16-beat cycles (tintal) of evenly balanced sets of four beats. Against this the sarangi's rhythms become increasingly complex, with many irregular groups of fast-moving notes.

Rhythms in the Berlioz are straightforward with the saltarello dance so prominent. This is a lively dance from the south of Italy, and here Berlioz uses the typical dotted-rhythm figures. The *Serenade* is much calmer, and gives us a peaceful interlude in a contrasting style. The Cage is the most complex of the three as its time signature is constantly changing, and there are all sorts of contrasting groups, e.g. triplets, quintuplets, septuplets, etc.

Examiner's points

The credit-worthy points were as follows:

➤ Drones in both *Harold in Italy* and *Rag Bhairav* (credit for both, with illustrated point for *Rag Bhairav*)

➤ Accept the point about the drones in Sonata III (location given)

➤ Chord G^7 at the start of Sonata I (illustrated point)

➤ Parallel chords in Sonata I (illustrated point, but not located)

➤ Free ad-libbing in the first section of *Rag Bhairav* (not precisely located)

➤ More rhythmic activity at the entry of the tabla (location given)

➤ 16-beat tintal

➤ Irregular groups of fast-moving notes (illustrated point)

➤ Saltarello dance rhythms in *Harold in Italy* (not located)

➤ Changing time signatures in the Sonatas (not located)

➤ Triplets, quintuplets and septuplets in the Sonatas (not located).

The essay was not very well-organised, and not all of the 12 points made were properly illustrated or located. It seemed that the candidate was attempting some interesting comparisons at the outset, but the attempt was largely unsuccessful because of the lack of system and detailed information. The work falls into the 'adequate' category and would receive **19/36**.

Exercise

Re-organise the essay above so that the information is presented in a much more systematic manner. Find examples to substantiate the un-illustrated points.

Glossary

This glossary is not comprehensive: it refers to terms as used in this volume. For more information about harmonic terms (e.g. suspension) see the AS Harmony Workbook *and/or the* A2 Harmony Workbook *by Hugh Benham (Rhinegold Education, 2008). For fuller definitions of other terms and expressions consult the* Dictionary of Music in Sound *by David Bowman (Rhinegold Education, 2002).*

Acciaccatura. A very short ornamental note played before a principal melodic note, written or printed as ♪.

Additive rhythm. Where a bar has beats of unequal length, or where unequal short rhythmic sets are grouped together to form a longer rhythmic pattern.

Aeolian mode. A scale that uses the following pattern of tones (T) and semitones (s): T–s–T–T–s–T–T. When starting on A, it consists of all the white notes within one octave on a keyboard.

Alberti bass. A particular type of broken-chord pattern often found in classical keyboard music with three pitches heard in the order low-high-middle-high, e.g. C–G–E–G.

Anacrusis. Note or notes preceding the first beat of a piece or phrase.

Angular. When applied to melody, the presence of wide leaps.

Anthem. A type of church music for choir, often accompanied by organ, and occasionally by larger forces. An anthem usually has English words (often from the Bible).

Antiphony. Performance by different singers/instrumentalists in alternation. Often – but not always – the different groups perform similar material.

Appoggiatura. A non-chord note that sounds on the beat as a dissonance and then resolves by step (up or down) to the main chord note. The dissonant note is not 'prepared' as a suspension is. Although appoggiaturas are normally approached by leap, accented passing notes that are particularly long and/or prominent are often described as appoggiaturas, even though they are approached by step. Sometimes an appoggiatura, especially in the Classical period, is indicated by a note in small type, followed by its resolution printed at normal size.

Arco. A direction to bow notes on a string instrument.

Aria. A song (usually from an **opera**, oratorio or **cantata**) for solo voice, plus accompaniment for orchestra or, sometimes in Baroque times, for smaller forces, even just **continuo**. An aria often provides a character in an opera with the opportunity to reflect at length on their emotional state.

Articulation. The manner in which a series of notes are played with regards to their separation or connection – for example, staccato (separated) or legato (connected).

Atonal. Atonal music avoids keys or modes; that is, no pitch stands out consistently in the way that the tonic does in tonal music.

Augmentation. The lengthening of the rhythmic values of a previously-heard melody (e.g. where ♩ ♫ has become 𝅗𝅥 ♩ ♩).

Augmented triad. A three-note chord in which the interval between successive notes is a major 3rd; for example, the chord D–F♯–A♯.

Augmented 6th chord. A chromatic chord which in root position spans the interval of an augmented 6th, e.g. A♭–F♯.

Bebop. A style of jazz that developed in the 1940s from swing. More complex and less easy to dance to, it was characterised by **improvisation**, fast tempos, irregular phrase lengths and a greater emphasis on the rhythm section.

Binary form. A structure consisting of two sections, the first of which closes in a related key and the second in the t onic. This structure was frequently used by Baroque composers, e.g. in dance movements.

Bitonal. Music that uses two different keys simultaneously.

Broken chord. The performing of the notes of a chord one after another instead of simultaneously.

Cadence. A pair of chords signifying the end of a phrase in tonal music. Cadences are of several types, of which perfect and imperfect are by far the most common. *See also* **Imperfect cadence, Interrupted cadence, Perfect cadence, Plagal cadence** and **Phrygian cadence**.

Cadential 6–4. Chord Ic, preceding chord V or V^7 in a perfect or imperfect cadence.

Calypso. A genre of song from Trinidad characterised by humorous or subversive lyrics. The music itself merges European and African elements.

Cambiata. Generally used to describe the movement from an unaccented non-harmony note which is quitted by a leap of a 3rd.

Canon. A strict form of **imitation**, in which each successive part repeats exactly the music of the first part.

Cantata. Most commonly a work for voice(s) and instruments in several movements, with **aria**(s), **recitative**(s) and chorus(es). A cantata can be sacred or secular.

Cantus firmus. An already existing melody (frequently plainchant or a **chorale**) to which other freely composed parts are added to make a new piece.

Chorale. A German hymn of the kind sung in the Lutheran (Protestant) church in the time of J. S. Bach. The word 'chorale' can refer to the words only, to the associated melody only, or to the whole hymn. Chorale melodies are largely stepwise (or **conjunct**); their harmonisation has long featured in advanced music courses.

Chordal. A form of homophony in which all the parts move together in the same or very similar rhythm. The term **homorhythmic** (literally 'same rhythm') is sometimes used instead.

Chromatic. A chromatic note is one that does not belong to the scale of the key currently in use. For example, in D major the notes G♯ and C♮ are chromatic. Music that is chromatic contains many chromatic notes.

Circle of 5ths. A harmonic progression in which the roots of the chords move by descending 5ths (and/or ascending 4ths), e.g. B–E–A–D–G–C etc.

Coda. A concluding section of a movement.

Comping. A term associated with jazz and popular music referring to the playing of a **chordal** accompaniment.

Compound time. A metre in which the main beat is subdivided into three equal portions, as opposed to two equal portions in **simple time**.

Concerto. Most commonly, a work for a soloist with orchestra. In many concertos the solo instrument is a piano or violin. Occasionally there may be two soloists (a double concerto) or even three (a triple concerto). (In the 17th century the term was used more widely, and was applied originally to a work in which voices and instruments, with more or less independent parts, collaborated in a manner that was new at the time.) *See also* **Concerto grosso**.

Concerto grosso. A type of concerto, most common in the late Baroque period, in which three (or occasionally more) soloists, known as the 'concertino', are contrasted with the sound of a larger group of mainly string instruments, know as the 'ripieno'.

Conjunct. Melodic movement by step rather than by leap. Opposite of **disjunct**.

Continuo. Short for 'basso continuo', the continuo instruments form the accompaniment in Baroque music. It may include instruments such as the harpsichord (capable of playing full harmony) and a cello or bassoon reinforcing the bass line.

Contrapuntal. Adjective to describe music that uses **counterpoint**.

Counterpoint. Counterpoint involves two or more melodic lines (usually rhythmically contrasted), each significant in itself, which are played or sung together at the same time. The term polyphonic is often used as a synonym for contrapuntal.

Counter-subject. In a fugue, the melodic material that is heard in counterpoint with the answer.

Cross rhythm. The use of two or more very different rhythms simultaneously in different parts. One rhythm may imply one metre (or time signature), while another implies a different one.

Development. The central part of a **sonata form** movement between the **exposition** and the recapitulation, containing a working-out of ideas already heard in the exposition.

Dialogue. When two or more instruments or voices have a musical 'conversation', with the individual parts responding to one another.

Diatonic. Using notes that belong to the current key. A diatonic note is one that belongs to the scale of the key currently in use. For example, in D major the notes D, E and F♯ are diatonic.

Diminished 7th chord. A four-note chord made up of superimposed minor 3rds.

Diminished interval. An interval that is one semitone narrower than a minor or perfect interval. A diminished 4th (e.g. G♯–C) is one semitone narrower than a perfect 4th (G–C); a diminished 6th (e.g. B–G♭) is one semitone narrower than a minor 6th (B–G).

Diminution. The shortening of the rhythmic values of a previously-heard melody (e.g. where ♩ ♪ ♪ has become ♪ ♫).

Disjunct. Melodic movement by leap rather than by step. Opposite of **conjunct**.

Dissonance. Strictly speaking, any note not belonging to a triad in root position or first inversion (even the 4th above the bass in a second inversion counts as dissonant). Some dissonances, particularly suspensions and appoggiaturas, add tension, which in early music had to be 'resolved'; others, notably passing and auxiliary notes, provide rhythmic and melodic decoration.

Divertimento. A piece (most commonly from the 18th century) whose style is partly or wholly light and intended to 'divert' or 'amuse' listeners, perhaps at a social function. A divertimento is normally in several movements, with at least one in a dance (particularly minuet) style.

Dominant 7th chord. A four-note chord built on the dominant (fifth) note of the scale. It includes the dominant triad plus a minor 7th above the root.

Dorian mode. A scale that uses the following pattern of tones (T) and semitones (s): T–s–T–T–T–s–T. When starting on D, it consists of all the white notes within one octave on a keyboard.

Double-stopping. The playing of two notes simultaneously on adjacent strings of a string instrument. The term is sometimes used loosely to cover three- and four-note multiple stopping. See also **Triple-stopping**.

Drone. A sustained note (or notes frequently forming an interval of a 5th) held in one part while other parts play or sing melodies against it.

Dynamics. How loudly or softly the music is played; the volume of the music. Indicated by dynamic markings such as *piano* (quiet) and *crescendo* (gradually get louder).

Exposition. The first section of a **sonata form** movement, typically including the first subject in the tonic and the second subject in a related key.

Fall off. In jazz, a short downward slide ending in silence.

False relation. The occurrence of the ordinary and chromatically altered versions of the same note (such as F♮ and F♯) in two different parts at the same time, or in close proximity.

Figured bass. A figured bass is an instrumental bass part with 'figures' or 'figuring' (chiefly numerals and sharp, flat and natural signs) designed to show a continuo keyboard or lute player what type of chord to play.

First inversion. *See* **Inversion**.

Fortspinnung. The spinning out of a melody line typically by repetition, sequence, variation of intervals, inversion, etc. The term is frequently applied in analysis of Baroque music.

Fractal scheme. A term sometimes used to describe Cage's 'micro-macrocosmic' structures: a self-symmetrical scheme in which each segment is a miniature version of the whole.

Fragmentation. The splitting up of melodic lines into shorter components, which are then treated in isolation.

Fugal. *See* **Fugue**.

Fugato. A passage in **fugal** style which forms part of a larger of music.

Fugue. A type of piece in which a main theme called a 'subject' is treated in imitation

by all the parts. 'Episodes' are the contrasting sections which depart from this pattern.

Functional harmony. A type of harmony that gravitates to the tonic through use of a hierarchy of chords, the dominant being second only to the tonic, and cadences.

Galliard. A fast triple-time dance of the Renaissance era, usually consisting of three repeated sections (A A, B B, C C). It was frequently paired with a **pavan(e)**.

Gamelan. An ensemble from Indonesia (usually Bali or Java) consisting largely of tuned percussion.

Ghost note. In jazz, a note that is deliberately played so faintly as to be almost inaudible.

Gigue. A quick, lively Baroque dance commonly in compound time, it was one of the key components of a Baroque (dance) suite.

Glissando. A slide from one pitch to another.

Gongan. In **gamelan** music, a rhythmic unit concluded by the sounding of the gong.

Half-valving. The partial opening of a valve on a brass instrument to result in a weak tone and unfocused pitch. The technique is particularly used in jazz.

Harmonics. A technique of lightly touching the string (e.g. on a violin) to produce a high, flute-like sound.

Head. In jazz and popular music, the basic substance of the number which is then varied. The structure is sometimes referred to as a head arrangement.

Hemiola. The articulation of two units of triple time (strong–weak–weak, strong–weak–weak) as three units of duple time (strong–weak, strong–weak, strong–weak).

Heterophony. A type of texture in which a melody is performed simultaneously with one or more rhythmically and/or melodically varied versions of itself.

Homophony. A texture in which one part has a melody and the other parts accompany, in contrast to contrapuntal writing, where each part has independent melodic and rhythmic interest.

Homorhythm. *See* **Chordal.**

Idée fixe. A term associated originally with Berlioz's music, signifying a recurring musical **motif.**

Imitation. Where a melodic idea in one part is immediately repeated in another part (exactly or inexactly), at the same or a different pitch, while the first part continues. Described with the adjective imitative.

Imperfect cadence. An open-ended cadence in which the dominant chord (V) is preceded by any other suitable chord, often I, ii or IV.

Impressionism. A compositional movement that began in France in the late 19th century and continued into the 20th, and was in some respects similar to the art movement of the same name. Important characteristics of impressionist music include heightened attention to timbre, colour and atmosphere, non-functional harmony and tonality and fluid metre.

Improvisation. Characteristic of jazz, the spontaneous creation of new music, often based on existing musical material (such as a chord pattern).

Incidental music. Music usually written for stage, film or television, which establishes an appropriate atmosphere for the action it accompanies.

Interrupted cadence. A cadence most frequently consisting of chords V–VI, designed to defeat expectations by avoiding chord I.

Inversion (harmonic). When a chord has a note other than the root in the lowest part, it is an inversion. In a first-inversion chord the 3rd of the chord is in the lowest part,

and in a second-inversion chord the 5th. For example, a triad of F major in first inversion is A–C–F, and in second inversion is C–F–A. *See also* **Root position.**

Inversion (melodic). When a melody line is heard upside down, e.g. pitches C–E–D are presented as C–A–B.

Inverted pedal. A pedal note which is held in a higher part of the texture, rather than in the bass.

Ionian mode. A scale that uses the following pattern of tones (T) and semitones (s): T–T–s–T–T–T–s. When starting on C, it consists of all the white notes within one octave on a keyboard.

Keteg. In **gamelan** music, individual rhythmic cells, the equivalent of bars, which together form the gongan.

Klangfarbenmelodie. German for 'sound-colour-melody'. A musical technique in which a melodic line is distributed among more than one instrument, thereby producing different timbres depending on which instruments are used.

Leading note. The seventh degree of a major or minor scale, usually with a strong tendency to rise to the tonic.

Leitmotif. A theme that is associated with a character, situation, mood, object or idea, especially in the operas of Richard Wagner and dramatic works/film music of later composers.

Libretto. The script or words for a dramatic work that is set to music (e.g. an opera, musical or oratorio).

Lydian mode. A scale that uses the following pattern of tones (T) and semitones (s): T–T–T–s–T–T–s. When starting on F, it consists of all the white notes within one octave on a keyboard. When the fourth is raised in a major scale, this is sometimes termed a Lydian inflection.

Melismatic. The setting of several notes to one syllable.

Melody-dominated homophony. A melody and accompaniment texture in which the accompaniment is not strictly chordal.

Metre. The metre refers to the pulse of the music and is indicated by the time signature.

Miniature. A short instrumental piece that depicts a scene or represents a mood.

Minimalism. A 20th- and 21st-century often deliberately simple style of composing based on repetitions of short melodic and rhythmic patterns. It was developed by American composers such as Steve Reich, Philip Glass and Terry Riley.

Modal. A term often used to refer to music based on a mode rather than on major and minor keys.

Modulation. A change of key, or the process of changing key.

Monody. A term used in connection with early Baroque music in particular, referring to a solo vocal line accompanied by continuo instruments only.

Monophony. Music consisting only of a single melodic line. Also described with the adjective 'monophonic'.

Motet. A type of church music for choir, sometimes accompanied by organ, and occasionally by larger forces. A motet often has Latin words (commonly from the Bible), and is particularly but not exclusively associated with Roman Catholic services. Motets were often composed for specific occasions, unlike the Ordinary of the Mass.

Motif. A short but distinctive musical idea that is developed in various ways in order to create a longer passage of music. The adjective is 'motivic'.

Neapolitan 6th chord. A chromatic chord (often in a minor key) consisting of the first inversion of the major chord formed on the flattened supertonic, i.e. the second degree of the scale (in D minor, for example, the Neapolitan 6th has the notes G–B♭–E♭).

Neoclassical. In music the adjective 'neoclassical' is most widely applied to certain early and mid 20th-century styles that combine a clear debt to previous eras (notably the Baroque and the Classical) with more up-to-date elements.

Obbligato. A prominent (and essential – 'obligatory') instrumental part in Baroque music, often in an aria, in addition to the vocal part and **continuo**.

Opera. A large-scale dramatic work for singers and instrumentalists in which the whole text is sung.

Ornamentation. Addition of melodic decoration, often through the use of conventional forms such as trills and mordents.

Ostinato. A repeating melodic, harmonic or rhythmic motif, heard continuously throughout part or the whole of a piece.

Parallelism. Also known as parallel harmony, this is the parallel movement of two or more melodic lines or chords.

Passing note. A non-harmony note approached and quitted by step in the same direction, often filling in a melodic gap of a 3rd (e.g. A between G and B, where both G and B are harmony notes).

Pavan(e). Slow, quadruple-time dance of the Renaissance era, usually consisting of three repeated sections (A A, B B, C C).

Pedal (note). A sustained or repeated note, usually in a low register, over which changing harmonies occur. A pedal on the fifth note of the scale (a dominant pedal) tends to create a sense of expectation in advance of a perfect cadence; a pedal on the keynote (a tonic pedal) can create a feeling of repose.

Pelog. In gamelan music, a seven-note scale. Often, only five notes from such a scale are actually used.

Pentatonic. A scale made up of five notes, most frequently the first, second, third, fifth and sixth degrees of a major scale (for example, C pentatonic is C–D–E–G–A).

Perfect cadence. A cadence consisting of the dominant chord (V or V^7) followed by the tonic (I).

Periodic phrasing. In Classical-period music particularly, where phrases of regular length are heard in balanced structures. The expression 'antecedent and consequent' is sometimes applied to these phrases.

Phrygian cadence. A type of imperfect cadence, in which the dominant chord (V) is preceded by the first inversion of the subdominant (IVb). It is used chiefly in minor keys, and particularly in Baroque music.

Pitch bend. In jazz, a microtonal variation in pitch.

Pizzicato (often abbreviated to **pizz.**). A direction to pluck, instead of bow, string(s) on a violin, viola, cello or double bass. Cancelled by the direction '**arco**' – with the bow.

Plagal cadence. A cadence consisting of the subdominant chord followed by the tonic (IV–I).

Pointillism. Originally referring to a painting technique, in which small dots of colour are carefully placed to create a larger image, this refers to a musical effect in which different notes are played or sung in isolation from each other, rather than as part of a musical line, thereby sketching out a larger musical form.

Polyphony. Sometimes used as an alternative term for **counterpoint**, especially in relation to Renaissance music.

Polyrhythm. The use of more than one rhythm at the same time, often implying the presence of different metres.

Post-modernism. A style of composition that deliberately contrasts itself with modernist concepts, and the highly intellectual approach (typified by serialism) associated with them. Post-modernism tries to avoid categorising music rigidly, and

often incorporates fragments of works and references to other cultures in a more approachable style.

Prime order. In **serialism**, the original order in which the notes of a tone-row are played.

Programmatic. Music with a stimulus that comes from outside the music itself.

Quartal harmony. Harmony based on the interval of a 4th (e.g. with chords such as A–D–G), rather than on the interval of a 3rd as in triads and 7th chords.

Quarter tone. Half a semitone.

Recapitulation. In **sonata form**, the section which follows the **development**. It is often closely based on the **exposition**, but normally both opens and closes in the tonic key.

Recitative. A piece for solo voice in an **opera, cantata** or oratorio (often before an **aria**) in which clear projection of words is the main concern. In many recitatives the music is functional rather than of great interest in itself, with the accompaniment often just for **continuo**.

Retrograde. The pitches of a previously heard melody or rhythm presented in reverse order.

Riff. In popular music styles, a short repeating phrase.

Ritornello form. A structure used in Baroque music in which an opening instrumental section (called the ritornello) introduces the main musical ideas. This returns, often in shortened versions and in related keys, between passages for one or more soloists. The complete ritornello (or a substantial part of it) returns in the tonic key at the end.

Rondo. A form in which the main theme (or subject) returns periodically in the tonic key. Simple rondo takes the form A–B–A–C–A etc., while Sonata rondo involves recapitulation of a second subject as well as the first: A–B(related key)–A–C(development)–A–B(tonic)–A. This form came to be used frequently in finales.

Root position. A chord that has the root in the lowest sounding part.

Rounded binary form. A variation of simple **binary form** (AB), in which a thematic reference to the beginning of the moment is made at the end of the B section.

Rubato. The variation of pulse by subtle lengthening and shortening of notes, so producing a free rhythmic feel.

Saltarello. A lively dance in $\frac{6}{8}$ which originated from Naples in the 13th century.

Scherzo. A fast movement which eventually replaced the minuet of the Classical era.

Secondary dominant. A passing or temporary dominant hinting at a different key, e.g. in C major, an E major chord acting as dominant to a tonic of A minor.

Secondary 7th. A 7th chord built on a degree of the scale other than the dominant.

Second inversion. *See* **Inversion.**

Sequence. Immediate repetition of a melodic or harmonic idea at a different pitch.

Serial. In serial music all (or most) pitches are derived from an underlying fixed series of pitches that can be manipulated by transposition, inversion and retrograding (being played backwards). A widely practised form of serialism in the mid 20th century used a series (or 'row') of twelve notes that included every note of the chromatic scale once.

Simple time. A metre in which the main beat is sub-divided into two equal portions. Opposite of **compound time.**

Sonata. An instrumental work, commonly in three or four movements. From the late Baroque period onwards, sonatas are usually for solo keyboard or for single melody instrument and keyboard. 'Trio sonatas' (middle to late Baroque) are normally for two violins and continuo.

Sonata form. Typical first movement form of the Classical and Romantic periods. In three sections – **exposition, development, recapitulation** – often based on two groups of melodic material in two contrasting keys (first subject, second subject).

Stretto. The overlapping of imitative entries more closely than had previously occurred, used especially in connection with **fugal** writing.

Stride. A jazz piano style partly derived from ragtime, in particular from the characteristic left-hand pattern which repeatedly 'strides' from a low note or chord on a strong beat to an often much higher chord on a weak beat. Stride piano was especially popular in the 1920s.

Substitution chord. A chord that is substituted for another chord for the sake of variety. In particular the term is used in jazz.

Suspension. A suspension occurs at a change of chord, when one part hangs on to (or repeats) a note from the old chord, creating a clash, after which the delayed part resolves by step (usually down) to a note of the new chord.

Swung rhythm. In jazz and other popular music, a certain freedom in performance whereby rhythms that might in other contexts be played 'straight' as equal notes are performed with the first of each pair longer than the second, often giving a kind of triplet effect.

Syllabic. The setting of one note to one syllable.

Symphony. A work for orchestra with several (usually three or four) movements in different tempi – in effect a sonata for orchestra rather than for one or a few instruments.

Syncopation. The shifting of stress from a strong to a weak beat. For example, in a $\frac{4}{4}$ bar with the rhythm ♩ ♩ ♩, the minim (a relatively long note beginning on a weak beat) is syncopated.

Ternary form. A musical structure of three sections in which the outer sections are similar and the central one contrasting (ABA).

Tertiary progression. When roots of chords or key areas proceed by 3rds.

Tessitura. A specific part of a singer's or instrument's range. For example a 'high tessitura' indicates a high part of the range.

Texture. The relationship between the various simultaneous lines in a passage of music, dependent on such features as the number and function of the parts and the spacing between them.

Through-composed. Applied to music in which the composer avoids repetition of previous material, i.e. fresh material for different phrases in a vocal work.

Tierce de Picardie. A major 3rd in the final tonic chord of a passage in a minor key.

Timbre. The element of music concerned with the actual sound quality, or tone colour, of the music.

Tonality. Music is described as being tonal when one note is of central importance, other notes being subordinate. The note of central importance is termed the tonic when major and minor keys and scales are used. In 18th-and 19th-century music tonality is established and maintained by functional harmony, but tonality can be based instead on other types of scales, notably modes.

Transition. A linking passage.

Tremolo. A rapid and continuous repetition of a single note or two alternating notes.

Trill. An ornament in which two adjacent notes rapidly and repeatedly alternate (the note bearing the trill sign and the one above it). The symbol for trill is *tr*.

Trio sonata. A musical form prevalent in the Baroque era, a trio sonata is written for two solo melody instruments and basso continuo, making three parts in total (hence the name 'trio' sonata); however, the continuo part would normally have had two or more instruments playing, usually a cello or bass viol and a harpsichord.

Triple-stopping. The playing of three notes simultaneously (or as near simultaneously as possible) on adjacent strings of a string instrument. *See also* **Double-stopping.**

Triplet. A group of three equal notes played in the time normally taken by two notes of the same type.

Tritone. An interval that is equivalent to three tones (an augmented 4th or dimished 5th).

Turn. A four-note ornament that 'turns' around the main note. It starts on the note above, drops to the main note, drops to the note below and then returns to the main note. Indicated by the symbol ∞.

Twelve-bar blues. A standard chord sequence used in the blues and other popular music, which is based on the tonic (I), subdominant (IV) and dominant (V) chords of a key. Its most common form is I–I–I–I, IV–IV–I–I, V–IV–I–I.

Unison. Simultaneous performance of the same note or melody by two or more players or singers.

Walking bass. A bass part that persistently uses the same note length.

Whole-tone scale. A scale in which the interval between every successive note is a whole tone.